T0350856

BOCCONI
UNIVERSITY
PRESS

Maria Giovanna Onorati

THE WHY BEHIND THE FOOD BUY

Contradictions of Food Consumption amid Changing Times

Cover: Cristina Bernasconi, Milan
Typesetting: Imagine, Trezzo sull'Adda (Mi)

EGEA S.p.A.
Via Salasco, 5 - 20136 Milano
Tel. 02/5836.5751 – Fax 02/5836.5753
egea.edizioni@unibocconi.it – www.egeaeditore.it

First edition: September 2024

ISBN Domestic Edition	979-12-80623-08-9
ISBN International Edition	978-88-31322-79-9
ISBN Digital Domestic Edition	978-88-238-8892-0
ISBN Digital International Edition	979-12-81627-80-5

Stampa: Geca Industrie Grafiche, San Giuliano Milanese (Mi)

MISTO
Carta | A sostegno della
gestione forestale responsabile
FSC   FSC® C007287

Questo libro è stampato su carta FSC® amica delle foreste. Il logo FSC® identifica prodotti che contengono carta proveniente da foreste gestite secondo i rigorosi standard ambientali,economici e sociali definiti dal Forest Steward Ship Council® e altre fonti controllate.

Table of Contents

Part II. What Do We Eat Today?
Old and New Eating Dilemmas in Times of Crisis

Part III. We Eat What We Would Like to Be Like

Introduction
The Unpostponable Call for a Change of the Production/Consumption Paradigm in Times of Permanent Crisis

While I write the introduction to this book, Europe is being swept by a wave of revolts led by farmers and producers. In France, tractors occupy the outskirts in protest against new taxes on fossil fuels and rising production prices. Similarly, in Germany, protests by over 10,000 farmers erupt as the government decides to reintroduce previously suspended agricultural taxes and cut subsidies on diesel fuel for agricultural vehicles. In Poland, farmers, aboard tractors, have taken to the streets to protest against certain measures that appear to harm local agriculture. In recent years, farmers across Western Europe have become increasingly vocal in expressing their opposition to environmental protection measures they deem too costly. Notably, this turmoil against the expenses associated with European Union (EU) greener farming policies predate both the pandemic and the energy crisis, leaving many farmers struggling financially. The Netherlands witnessed particularly strong reactions when a 2019 court ruling on nitrogen emissions (accounting for about 4% of global greenhouse gas emissions, according to FAO) sparked ongoing protests immediately labeled as farmers' resistance against government attempts to shut down farms and decrease the number of animals. In Belgium, similar challenges last March resulted in convoys of tractors congesting the EU quarter in Brussels. In Ireland, while the protests have been smaller, dairy farmers upset about nitrogen restrictions marched with their cows to the offices of three government ministers last month. Spain and Greece have also experienced similar turmoils.

Next to these protests specifically aimed at contesting the economic impact of EU greener measures, there are also those that oppose the massive imports of agricultural products from Ukraine flooding the Polish and the Romanian markets, also jeopardizing the profitability of local production. Romanian farmers, along with truck drivers, are blocking the borders with Ukraine, in revolt against the excessively cheap Ukrainian wheat. This is also the effect of EU's decision in June 2022, to liberalize trade with Ukraine in the effort to mitigate the impact on Kyiv's agricultural sector caused by the prolonged war. These farmers' uprisings do not stem from anti-European or anti-ecologist sentiments. Instead, they arise in response to the exclusionary impacts of agricultural policies that, despite being moved by the best intentions, likely lack a genuine forward-looking approach demanded by sustainable development. The pressing and unpostponable need for ecological transition is proving that it cannot be met with short-term subsidy cuts, which are inevitably destined to short-term diminish yields and significantly affect production profitability. Likewise, the undisputable support to a nearby population and economy, like Ukraine's, devastated by a violent aggression needs a more far-looking approach than decisions leading to an influx of low-cost goods into the internal market of the EU, which would inevitably have impacted the profitability of local productions.

Obviously, the reasons for these protests as well as for price rise are more intricate than this oversimplification implies. Likewise, the social world where these dynamics occur is much more complex than this cognitive shortcut might suggest.

While each protest is fueled by diverse motivations deeply intertwined with national policies, they are united by one element: The divergence between, on the one hand, the imperative need for expeditiously advancing the ecological transition to a sustainable production and consumption paradigm, necessitating a comprehensive and nonnegotiable approach to change, which includes necessary restrictions. On the other hand, a dire crisis that encompasses the economic, energy, health, geopolitical, and social dimensions, demanding immediate actions to mitigate the inevitable costs of change, often conflicting with the imperatives of the ecological transition. This divergence is poised to manifest as an even more worrying overarching polarization lending itself to easy political exploitation and crystallizing into ideological positions.

It is the case of the increasingly pronounced supremacist rhetoric of the divergence between national interests and supranational policies (in this case attributed to the EU), upon which right-wing sovereigntists and populists are stoking the flames to gain electoral advantages, inflating anti-European sentiments, rising nationalism with the aim of accelerating opposition against the EU establishment.

The rise of the rural populist party "Farmer-Citizen Movement" in the Netherlands and the flag "Committee of Betrayed Farmers," under which Italian farmers united, staging protests against a rather indistinct range of issues, including taxes, diesel, land selloffs, insect flours, and cultivated meat, serve as examples. The "tricky" rhetoric appropriating these revolts and imbuing them with Eurosceptic sentiment is that of *the poor farmers being damaged and ignored by the rich, supranational elites (read "EU") with ideological (read: "hypocritical") vision of protecting the planet (read "obscure interests of global powers"), rather than the people who, through hard work, bring fresh food to our tables.*

The turn these revolts are taking goes beyond Euroscepticism; it tells a broader global story: a paradoxical dual forking between security and ecological transition. This is paradoxical because the challenges of a forward-looking approach demanded by sustainable development end up in a backward-looking response leveraging securitarian claims.

How does all of this relate to consumer choices? Despite the lengthy introduction, which unmistakably reflects the author's perspective, the intention of this book is not to embark on a critical discussion about the global crisis and the diverse economic, political, and geopolitical factors contributing to the fragmentation of the world's global order as known until now. However, transitioning toward a responsible production/consumption paradigm, as suggested by ecological thinking, involves adopting a comprehensive, "feedbacking" epistemological standpoint (Marten, 2001). This recognizes that actions in the realm of production have inevitable consequences on consumption, and vice versa, like a feedback loop.

It is estimated that food production is responsible for a quarter of global greenhouse gas emissions and that 21% of emissions come from the cultivation of crops intended for direct human consumption and 18% of emissions come from the supply chains where farm produce is processed into final products for consumption. This means that human food consumption accounts for between 20% and 40% of the total environmental impact (Ritchie, 2019). Urgent measures are required to address this situation. However, from a comprehensive perspective, one cannot ignore that the summing up of decisions to reduce reliance on pesticides and fertilizers, cut subsidies for agricultural diesel, and favor low-cost imports of staple foods, while each individually pointing to a desirable sustainable and inclusive development paradigm, would increase production costs in the short term, reduce the competitiveness of local products, and lead to higher food prices, challenging both producer and consumer agency. These first considerations about the connection to consumer choices allow an understanding that decisions made at various levels, from agricultural practices to economic policies, can ultimately influence the choices and affordability of consumers in the food market.

In this perspective, the question about what all of this has to do with a book investigating the reasons for food purchases takes probably relevance.

Straddling the line between serving as a manual for a sociological study of the diverse sociocultural dynamics sustaining food consumption and a broader reflection on the intricate and often contradictory sets of values and beliefs associated with eating during transition times, this book cannot overlook the complex scenario in which this reflection begins and develops. In the aftermath of the Weberian lesson, to understand why people act the way they do, means grasping the historical forces that, if not shaping their actions directly, have at least influenced the historical contexts in which they operated. In this book, sociological argumentation delves into the understanding of why we choose the foods we eat in the peculiar context of troubled and uncertain times – a question that unveils numerous others, including "why do we not consume the food we should?" or "why do we consume the food we shouldn't?" and so forth.

This purpose aligns with Weber's advocacy of a sociological standpoint, which connects cultural events to their concrete, historical causes through the study of precise data selected from particular perspectives. In own words, pronounced a century ago but never more relevant than today:

> Our aim is the understanding of the characteristic uniqueness of the reality in which we move. We wish to understand on the one hand the relationships and the cultural significance of individual events in their contemporary manifestations and on the other the causes of their being historically so and not otherwise (Weber, 2011 [1922], p. 72).

Long before farmer revolts swept across Europe, a global emergency unfolded in January 2020 with the outbreak of the pandemic, ushering in a state of initially acute and then normalized uncertainty known as the "new normal." This enduring period has brought forth prolonged challenges, including those posed by a partially subdued yet mysterious virus. It was accompanied by supply-chain disruptions and followed by a raw materials crisis worsened by subsequent wars. As a direct consequence of these wars, an energy shock spawned across Europe, which was largely dependent on energy sources held by countries in conflict. Economic volatility, unpredictable fluctuations, rising inflation, social tensions (including farmer protests), and escalating political turmoil stemming from these situations further contribute to featuring this crisis as a particularly multifaceted one. This sustained period of instability earned the appellation "permacrisis," a designation that would be entitled as the word of the year for 2022 by Collins Dictionary.[1]

The "perfect storm" of climate change, health emergencies, humanitarian catastrophes, energy shocks, and economic crises has given rise to various forms of upheaval, compromising the ecological transition and exacerbating its perceived divergence from security. At the same time, this utter tempest revealed the paramount importance of food, particularly food security, in the midst of a crisis.

In the context of this study, we will particularly analyze food and the challenges affecting it in current critical times from the perspective of consumption. Critics of this book will express their disappointment with the title itself, arguing that food-related consumption extends far beyond the act of purchase, and they are correct. Conversely, enthusiasts will appreciate that we start with the purchase because, especially in times of profound and prolonged crisis, this act encapsulates fundamental social dynamics. These dynamics encompass not only economic reasons or seemingly rational decisions but also symbolic, cultural, and social dimensions that involve consumers and their deepest beliefs in the broadest sense. As Bourdieu himself highlights in his seminal work framing the symbolic, distinctive meaning of consumer practices, most of the sociological significance of consumption as a lifestyle and expressions of taste and habitus revolves around and becomes manifest in the decisions surrounding the very act of purchase:

> Having a million does not in itself make one able to live like a millionaire; and parvenus generally take a long time to learn that what they see as cul-

---

[1] See: https://blog.collinsdictionary.com/language-lovers/a-year-of-permacrisis/ (accessed 30/04/2024).

pable prodigality is, in their new condition, expenditure of basic necessity. (Bourdieu, 1984, p. 374)

As implied by its title, this book sets out to engage in an explanatory inquiry about the "why," which remains a paramount concern for sociologists – still torn between "comprehending" and "explaining" (Fornari, 2002; Coenen-Huter, 2019). Nevertheless, this explanatory effort holds great importance also for marketers, advertisers, and various scholars and professionals navigating the intricate landscape of consumption, especially in disruptive times like the present.

By exploring the "why behind," this analysis invites readers to embark on a nuanced understanding of the intricate tapestry of concrete historical facts, considered as "clearly social," "socially relevant," and "socially conditioned" factors (to paraphrase the well-known Weberian tripartition) that shape our relationship with food as consumers in an ever-changing world. While our relationship with food has often been overlooked by the social sciences, particularly sociology, due to its seemingly trivial connection with bodily impulses and the "unreflective," taken-for-granted nature of our daily activities (Mennell et al., 1992, p. 1), it extends beyond mere "eating" and holds profound sociological significance. This significance emanates just from this deeply ingrained presence in our routines, addressing both basic nutritional needs and the more complex sphere of taste and preferences, which entail desires and lifestyles. Food-related routines become particularly crucial to comprehend, especially when disrupted, causing them to lose their unreflective feature. This is evident in the unprecedented centrality gained by food during crises, as illustrated above.

In recent years, food consumption, particularly of items with distinctive attributes (e.g., local, organic, and certified), has become a primary focus in consumer demands, marketers' discourses, and public narratives. This transformation serves as a mirror, reflecting more profound shifts in the social dynamics of our contemporary times, where food selecting has become a primary proof of consumer skills and discernment.

During periods of profound social change, when the predictive capabilities of expert systems weaken or falter, and perspectives become limited, the ability to seize glimpses of latent trends is not just an opportunity to undergo change but an extraordinary chance to actively influence and shape it. For instance, it becomes crucial not only to comprehend what consumers want and why but also to monitor their actions and formulate hypotheses about potential actions. This is essential in facilitating the alignment of supply with demand, representing a socially relevant strategy to counteract waste and losses. But also to let producers and brands to maintain a hold on post-traumatic stressed consumers.

The disruptions mentioned above have significantly reshaped consumer behaviors, leaving individuals overwhelmed by frequently conflicting and diverging tendencies. These changes prompt brands to incorporate them into their branding or rebranding strategies (Mintel, 2024a).

Examples of these conflicting sentiments include a renewed sense of "being human" emerging from widespread suffering caused by the pandemic and subsequent images of wars, clashing with a pervasive mistrust toward an unknown "other," evidenced by the rise of nationalist sentiments and sovereignty movements. The increasing nonmaterialistic desire for self-fulfillment, emphasizing values beyond monetary considerations, contrasts with a revengeful impulse toward consumption after an extended period of exclusion from it. The revival of communal relationships after social separation emerges alongside the simultaneous pervasive penetration of digital technologies and agile lifestyles developed during months of seclusion. A growingly polarized demand for engagement and stance-taking exists alongside a rising desire for relief from anxiety and an escape from mundane stressors. Similarly, an internalized new green awareness coexists with impoverishment and the loss of purchasing power, causing a delay or hindrance in adopting a greener lifestyle, aligning with the polarization highlighted in farmers' protests. An overarching sense of positive perspectives accompanies the mounting mental distress of post-traumatic consumers. The search for authenticity and security goes hand in hand with the pervasive influence of new artificial intelligence on consumers' daily lives and decisions in every aspect of their lives.

Such conflicting sentiments among consumers mirror, at the microlevel, the paradoxical divergence between security and sustainability emerging at the macro-level, as referred to at the beginning of this introduction, giving rise to contradictory axiology.

When navigating this intricate landscape, businesses must prioritize understanding and adapting to these evolving trends for resilience in these turbulent times. Additionally, with the aid of AI, they can propel the human-machine ecosystem toward co-creation (Euromonitor, 2024), establishing a new connection between production and consumption.

Global market insights underscore that manufacturers in the fast-moving consumer goods and consumer packaged goods (FMCG/CPG) sector, producing items intended for everyday consumer use with a short shelf life, have encountered three primary challenges since the onset of the pandemic: Recognizing shifts in consumer patterns and understanding their impact on short- and long-term demand, analyzing channel performance as shopping habits evolve, and comprehending consumers' motivations behind buying patterns (Nielsen, 2020). Even today, consumers around the world provide evidence that they want to connect with brands, and brands, in turn,

> [...] must reestablish and strengthen their relationship with consumers, placing consistent delivery of functionality at the core of their message and ensuring that reliability, trust and authenticity feed into the integrity of their identity and vision. (Mintel, 2024a)

Accordingly, the objective of this book is to lead readers through an exploration of the intricate interplay among societal, cultural, and individual influences that shape attitudes and choices in the realm of food consumption, particularly in this era marked by profound uncertainty. In alignment with its ambitious mission, the book delves into how sweeping societal transformations, unfolding amid a landscape of multiple crises, challenge individual eating habits, and mold them into new social configurations. The endeavor to explore and understand some of these challenges will be complemented by an effort to provide a comprehensive overview of prominent social theories that have examined the evolution of consumption, particularly in relation to food and taste, during key stages of modern and late modern society.

Chapter 1 provides an overview of consumption as a key concept in the social sciences and traces its evolution within the framework of the principal theoretical approaches and methodological analytical families, based on the categorization proposed by Halkier (2017), that have addressed it in the context of the rise and evolution of consumer society. This section explores the notion of the consumer as an agent in the market, which is itself viewed as a social space. The discussion centers around the analytical notion of "agency," referring to the subjective capacity to act – whether through actions or expressions – especially in relation to social change. This capacity can manifest as an individual's ability to effect change or resist structural constraints and social inertia, particularly during transitional periods aimed at developing a full awareness of responsible consumer behaviors as part of exercising citizenship. The section also reflects on how this concept of consumer agency has expanded in recent decades to encompass contrasting perspectives, particularly in light of post-anthropocentric perspectives that reconsider what it means to be human in a world where there is an increasing awareness of human impact on oneself and the surrounding environment. On the one hand, the proposed analysis emphasizes the importance of not disregarding the human subject and its capacity for self-reflection, focusing on values and individual empowerment through awareness, especially in consumption practices during times of crisis and social change. On the other hand, it includes theoretical formulations developed within a practice-theoretical perspective, such as the theory of dilemmas affecting consumer tastes amid an omnivorous offering. This formulation highlights agency less as an exercise of wholly intentional initiative and more as the performativity embedded in socially shaped practices that also influence tastes. While some consideration is given to these perspectives that underscore the diminishing role of individual intentionality in favor of a broader dynamic that includes the nonhuman realm, where both subjects and objects (such as technologies) act and are acted upon simultaneously, the text firmly advocates, from a sociological perspective, for maintaining a focus on the values that guide individuals to understand their contradictions, especially during times of transition.

Chapter 2 specifically examines food consumption through the lens of its contemporary dilemmas gripping consumers, underscoring the crucial role of sociological analysis in comprehending taste and its contradictions as a fundamental component of consumer culture and society, and its updating in light of an idea of sustainability that is increasingly elusive and contradictory. This section questions the feasibility of continuing to use antinomic categories, as introduced by Warde about thirty years ago, in a post-anthropocentric era where a holistic and ecological vision should negate any dualism. However, the analysis demonstrates that, just as nudges and technoscience have not reduced or eliminated human agency but instead have amplified it, similarly, the complexity and transcendence of an anthropocentric view, where humans act in opposition to a reified nature, have not eradicated dualisms. On the contrary, contemporary complexity is forcefully bringing them back into prominence through rhetoric that strongly emphasizes polarized stances' tracing the development of food antinomies to the present day and examinig the dilemmas faced by contemporary food consumers amid the crisis and their contradictory stances. Moving from the four basic antinomies devised by Alan Warde over twenty years ago and proposing an updated evolution, this section particularly explores how conflicting values, increasingly oscillating between environmental concerns and identity aspirations in a society that is in a permanent, multilayered crisis, can lead to sometimes paradoxical consumption choices.

Chapter 3 explores another dimension rooted in consumer dynamics, which the beyond-human dynamic of structure and agency, surpassing traditional human-centric views, has not yet disregarded: the aspirational side of consumption. "We eat what we would like to be like" reviews and subverts, in sociological terms, the overused philosophical statement "we are what we eat." It examines how consumers, in their practical choices, are guided not only by practical needs or interests but also by aspirations, desires, and the symbolic meanings attached to the products or experiences they consume. This desirability, far from being a "bias" in consumer choices, reflects the internalized value system distinguishing social groups and influences the "why" behind food purchases in terms of the stratification of tastes. In this section this dimension of consumption analysis encompasses the internalized material factors that shape consumer aspirations for social distinction through the exhibition of tastes, revealing their underlying social stratification. For example, this section focuses on how the ostentatious consumption once associated with wealthy consumers, as described by Veblen, has transformed into a middle-class pursuit of cultural refinement and skillful connoisseurship, often manifesting as competition with neighbors, as outlined by Bourdieu. A competition that remains vibrant despite the apparent disappearance of overt social conflicts continues to shape the contemporary foodscape. In this section, space is also devoted to the role of culture and symbolic meanings. Here, we find references to approaches emphasizing the cultural side of consumption, represented on the right-hand side of our chart depicting the analytical families of consumption (Figure 2).

Chapter 4 addresses consumption as a behavior, illustrated on the upper-left side of the analytical families. The approaches and examples provided in this chapter focus on the normative values internalized as

subjective motives in the form of attitudes and practical evaluative judgments that sustain decision-making, particularly in reference to sustainable consumer behaviors. By delving into the drivers of consumption,
aided by theoretical frameworks that account for the role of values and
sociocultural motives associated with eating habits, this part provides
an examination of the complex and contradictory axiology that shape
people's dietary choices amid changing social and cultural landscapes.
The reader is called to confront with a critical analysis of the intricacies
of contemporary consumer dynamics in a society that values both omnivorism with its compulsion to consume and sustainable eating with its
de-consumeristic call for frugality and mindfulness.

Focused on both consumer practices and behaviors, these two sections
offer a broad overview on different sociological understanding framing
both conventional and emerging forms of consumption from different
angles. The analysis presents various paradigms framing consumption
within the social sciences, including those by Veblen, Bourdieu, Warde,
Mennell, Maffesoli, Schwartz, Ajzen, and Durkheim, who, at the end
of the book, provides us with insights into social dynamics still valuable
for delving into the social forces at play in contemporary foodscapes. Actually, these paradigms represent the "chalk and cheese" (Shove, 2010,
p. 1279) of perspectives on consumption within the social sciences.
"Chalk" refers to theories focusing on causal factors and external drivers, treating habits as drivers of individual behavior or emphasizing the
meaning-making and symbolic side of agency. By contrast, "cheese" encompasses theories that place routines and socially shaped practices as
the central units of inquiry, emphasizing the endogenous and emergent
dynamics inscribed within them and effacing the agent to carriers of
performances. Indeed, all of them remain very powerful in addressing
different aspects of consumer patterns, which, in difficult and changing
times, are morphing into enigmatic and unpredictable forms. These paradigms help in finding suitable tools to decipher the mysteries behind the
"why" of food-buying decisions.

Furthermore, especially the reference to the concept of neotribe applied to the community creation dynamics online, the book doesn't overlook the influence of digital platforms and the proliferation of discourses about food on the formation of taste and identity, and the extent to
which digitalization contributes to creating duplicitous, contradictory
value systems and false but often appealing food mythologies (e.g., the

myth of "authentic food"). By examining the complex predicaments of sustainable eating in the digital environment, the analysis sheds light on the prevalence of elusive forms of food consumption practiced by increasingly unpredictable and disloyal consumers. These consumers are, nonetheless, actively seeking emotional resonance and value alignment with brands and social groups. Simultaneously, this section investigates the narrowing of socially desirable consumption patterns, wherein a subset of core values and predetermined scripts become indispensable for facilitating the urgent shift toward a sustainable paradigm. In this context, the evolving axiology related to food reveals the ambivalence inherent in the broader and contradictory, but no longer deferrable, process of embracing a greener culinary ethos. These aspects are focused on in the concluding chapter of the book, where some dynamics crucial in sociological thinking, namely the relationship between personal integration and social regulation of Durkheimian memory, are used to delve into the concept of authenticity – a paramount mantra for the contemporary food consumer. The quest for authenticity, crowding online and offline consumer claims, reflects the rise of communal feelings and new forms of imagined or practiced social attachment. These range from the (gastro)nationalistic drift behind the glorification of genuine local food to the online organization of networks for direct food purchases between farmers and consumers, representing a powerful paradigm shift toward sustainable consumption.

This exploration leaves the reader with an urgent and thought-provoking question going through the whole book since its cover: Is it possible, in an era marked by emerging "shocks" evolving into a permanent crisis, to catch some deeper explanatory patterns that may help understand and possibly reconcile the immediate concerns of the crisis agenda with the central and unpostponable imperatives of creating a more sustainable food system? No solution is of course provided, nor is it the intention. However, by employing the analytical lenses of sociological argumentation (and imagination), encouraging reflection to find explanatory connections, and raising awareness about some of the "whys" of current consumer trends, this exploration aims to pave the way for the initial question of *whether* a more sustainable future for foodscapes in an era marked by significant changes can be addressed, transforming it into the question of *how* it can be achieved. The decision of *when* and *wherefrom* to embark on this formidable journey lies with the reader.

Part I
Food Consumption in Changing Society

1   Eating as a Relevant Social Sphere of Action

1.1   Consumption as a key concept in the social sciences

Consumption stands as one of the most socially significant human activities. However, the early pioneers of sociology, such as Marx and Weber, only tangentially addressed consumption, with much of the initial sociological discourse on the consumption of goods emerging from economic analyses, exemplified by Veblen's examination of the leisure class. It wasn't until the mid-twentieth century that consumption became a central focus in the social sciences.

In his renowned work on consumption, English sociologist Alan Aldridge (2003) begins his analysis with the assertion that "Consumption is a "key concept" in the social sciences," suggesting its pivotal role in unlocking pathways to other fields and enabling exploration of new ones. According to Campbell (1995), consumption is defined as a process that

> involves the selection, purchase, use, maintenance, repair and disposal of any given product or service (Campbell, 1995, pp. 101–102).

This definition provides a neutral portrayal, capturing the broad function of consumption in consumer life. However, it falls short of conveying the immense significance of this term within the social sciences. Raymond Williams' historical examination of the term "consumer" (1976, pp. 78–79) reveals its pejorative origins dating back to the fourteenth century. Initially associated with notions of depletion, destruction, and wastefulness, "consumer" carried negative connotations, akin to terms like "use up," "destroy," "devour," and "waste." This negative association was so entrenched that "consumption" became synonymous with any wasting disease, including tuberculosis. Even in the nineteenth century, amid the dawn of modernity, "consumer" retained its unfavorable undertones, prompting the preference for "costumer" as an alternative term.

With the advent of bourgeois society, the term "consumer" sheds its pejorative connotations and assumes a neutral stance. However, classical analyses of capitalism exhibit a productivist bias, as noted by Scott (2011, p. 132), where the focal point is the "market subject" – whether depicted as the worker (Marx), the businessman (Weber), or the entrepreneur (Schumpeter) – rather than the consumer subject.

In the emerging framework of an organized market, the act of producing and utilizing goods begins to evoke the juxtaposition of two abstract entities: the "producer" and the "consumer," two interlinked yet opposing figures in the bourgeois economy. Within the pyramidal structure of early capitalism, consumption primarily served the interests of affluent groups and operated solely in function of production. While producers occupied a dominant position as purveyors of society's productivity and welfare, they also partook in consumption. However, the conspicuous consumption of goods, intended for display, remained the prerogative of either a leisured class inheriting privilege from aristocratic lineage or a burgeoning bourgeoisie emulating the patterns of the so-called leisure class by indulging in conspicuous consumption.

Marx was among the first to grasp this inherent contradiction between consumption and production within the capitalist system. His analysis underscores the imperative for the social sciences to delve beyond the realms of the market and mere purchase when exploring consumption.

In his *A Contribution to the Critique of Political Economy* (1859, Engl. edition 1904), the importance of consumption for the social sciences becomes clear. In his analysis of consumption, Marx emphasizes the interdependence between consumption and production, even delineating concepts such as "productive consumption" and "consumptive production" (p. 277). He highlights how production shapes consumption patterns and creates desires for its own products. Nevertheless, he also highlights how consumption ultimately completes the process by using and thus "destroying" the product, thereby validating both the product and the producer. In his own words:

Production produces consumption by a) creating the material; b) determining the mode of consumption; c) creating in the consumer a need for the objects which it first presents as products. It produces the object of consumption, the mode of consumption and the impulse of consumption. But consumption completes the product as a product by destroying it. Consumption is the final act that not only makes the product a product but also makes the producer a producer (pp. 179–180).

Despite consumption constituting the final phase of production, production maintains primacy within the economic cycle of early capitalism. However, Marx's critical analysis also acknowledges the inherent contradiction within the symbiotic relationship between consumption and production: Within capitalist society, the nexus between production and consumption is not direct but instead mediated by an external and autonomous force: The market. This conflicting situation eventually results in their disconnection, a destiny that consumer-driven societies would encounter a century later when consumerism began to rise (pp. 280–283).

1.2   From consumer to customer in the consumeristic society

It is only in the twentieth century that consumption becomes of paramount interest to the social sciences. This interest entails a focus on various aspects, including the social organization of personal resources to procure goods and services, the methods of procurement, and the utilization and enjoyment of these commodities, encompassing the social significance derived from such usage and enjoyment. Indeed, beyond mere consumption and consumers, it is consumerism – defined as the culture of consumption – that has assumed critical importance in the realm of social sciences.

Consumerism is the cultural expression of the divergence between production and consumption and of ubiquitous consumption as the epitome of a society that has made "consumer" and "consumption" dominant terms by which we conceptualize our relationship to all kinds of goods and services (Aldridge, 2003, p. 3) and that transformed the consumer into an abstract figure in an impersonal market.

The improvement of the average living conditions of people in capitalist societies led to an increase in consumption. This was one of the main consequences of the Fordist accumulation regime, in which the production system produced standardized, low-cost goods and paid its workers' wages sufficient to acquire these goods.

The contradiction was no longer between consumer and producer, whose relationship was entirely at the mercy of external market forces but between the "consumer" and the "customer."

The "customer," a figure who traditionally maintains an enduring personal relationship with a provider, represents in the twentieth century the commodification of the relationship between the subject and the products, which become commodities in market society.

The "customer" is therefore relegated to overtly commercial situations and replaced by the consumer, who became the preeminent figure in the mid-twentieth century because of his seemingly unverified agency and neutrality. Such neutrality is, of course, a deception, for when we consume, we position ourselves in social space. Consumption is a value-laden concept and therefore can never be neutral. It acquires a positive value when it is a path to comfort, prosperity, and satisfaction, while it acquires a pejorative meaning when it entails waste, extravagance, and selfishness.

The Fordist regime of accumulation, where consumption was still a function of what the system could materially produce, ended up when a flexible production emerged together with the ideal of an unlimited economic development that distinguishes mature capitalism. The emphasis on consumption became central, and consumption definitely separated from production. This trend in the economic cycle, known as Post-Fordism, has been described in several ways: the collapse of big social aggregates, the end of class structure, the diminishing of contrasts and the increase of differences, the rise of market segmentation into submarkets, and the explosion of niche consumption in the postmodern society.

Consumer behavior could no longer be understood simply as a response to the needs of new production techniques, nor could it be simply deduced from the greater variety of products, that firms can produce. Consumption becomes the expression of taste and indeed, along with the consumer, taste becomes a central category for understanding the aspirations of a consumeristic society. Consumerism refers not so much to usual behaviors but also to the mentality and even the ideology lying behind consumption. A mentality "assuming that such objects or recipes are essentially available; they may be obtained in exchange for money, and shopping is the way of obtaining them" (Aldridge, 2003, p. 4). In consumer(istic) societies, taste is a central concept for the social sciences and an orienting concept in everyday practice. Tastes become more determinate, more specialized, and more discriminating, since they manifest consumers' positioning within a vast range of supply, and the study of market needs shifts more and more toward the study of consumer culture and behavior to understand the proliferation of tasteful, symbolically recognizable, subcultural, consumption-based lifestyles.

Consumerism can be traced back to the early nineteenth century, when, with the rise of the Industrial Revolution in western societies, the amount of material goods being produced rose enormously at a cheaper price, thus becoming more accessible to many social groups and allowing them to increasingly engage in consumption. The first modern consumers were the upper classes and aristocracy, who were engaged in more and more leisure and expensive forms of consumption, so as to form the largest market for new luxury goods. Over the course of the nineteenth and twentieth centuries, conspicuous consumption spread to many more social groups, pushed to competition with upper classes by emulative impulses, and, by the mid-twentieth century, consumerism as a way of life characterized the developed economies.

1.3   Agency in consumeristic society

In social research, agency is a key concept often left untranslated in other languages due to its nuanced meaning, which brings us back to the core of sociology. Developed primarily within the Anglo-American sociological discourse on the phenomenology of action, agency is deeply rooted in power relations, highlighting the tension between individuals and societal structures with their coercive rules. In Europe, the concept of agency has been particularly discussed mainly in the context of the dualism between the self-determined individual and the socially determined structure (Rebughini, 2023). In fact, since its beginnings, sociology has been concerned with the factors that bind society together through centripetal forces, containing individual centrifugal tendencies. These collectively organized centripetal forces, functioning as social determinants that act upon individuals with the aim of preserving the societal framework, constitute the structure. Contrary to this, the individual's centrifugal will to act freely and liberate oneself from constraints is termed "agency." Spencer and Comte saw social structures as groups, collectives, and aggregates of individuals, but it was Durkheim's conception of social facts and of society as a distinct entity, outside and beyond the control of all individual intentions and purposes, which made the relationship between structure and the subject's agency a fundamental tension of sociological thought.

In general, agency represents a person's capacity for autonomous action, choice, and decision-making, as well as their ability to handle internalized forms of domestication. Most studies view the relationship between agency and structure as interrelated and recursive rather than oppositional (Giddens, 1984). According to the working definition provided by Giddens and Sutton (2014), structure/agency is:

> A conceptual dichotomy rooted in sociology's attempts to understand the relative balance between society's influence on the individual (structure) and the individual's freedom to act and shape society (agency) (Giddens and Sutton, 2014, pos. 642).

Although still entangled in the dualism of individual agency versus socially determined structure, agency is a polymorphic notion that remains at the heart of any framing of social theories today. In Western societies, agency has developed along three main dimensions: rationality, as an individual's capacity for decision-making where intentionality prevails, reflecting a Weberian legacy of "oriented" action; performativity of practices, where individuals enact and reproduce socially shaped activities; and self-reflexivity, where individuals are engaged in dialogic dynamics (Bratman, 2006).

Emirbayer and Mische (1998) perfectly capture this polymorphic nature by identifying three temporally structured components of agency: the past-oriented, reproducing "iterational element," which becomes the core of practice theory, namely, the "selective reactivation by actors of past patterns of thought and action, as routinely incorporated in practical activity" (Emirbayer and Mische, 1998, p. 971); the future-oriented "projective element," which encompasses the intentional-imaginative "generation by actors of possible future trajectories of action," contributing to the structuring power of agency in Giddens' theory; and the present-contextualized "practical-evaluative element," which involves individual actors making practical and value-based normative judgments among alternative trajectories in response to emerging demands and dilemmas.

Despite its widespread use, agency remains a complex and multifaceted concept that recalls the foundation of sociology, conceptualizing the relationship between the subject and the societal world. It continues to spark debates between different theoretical approaches, particularly functionalist and interactionist perspectives, and, more recently, between individualistic and practice-based formulations. These debates articulate subjects' engagement in actions as either performative, socially shaped practices or reflective evaluations, with the role of rationality remaining a subject of ongoing inquiry.

1.4   Ideal types of consumers between structure and agency

Consumption has been one of the favorite fields for sociological understanding of agency and its relationship with the constraints of structure (Warde, 2005). Whether it is a performance of internalized routines, as posited by practice theory, or an evaluative/intentional reflexivity upon actions, in consumer studies, agency primarily refers to the ability to act instrumentally, exerting one's influence and making decisions, though in a way that cannot be separated from its embeddedness in given rules, collectively shaped competencies and knowledge, and emotional patterns. In Western cultures, the archetype of the "consumer" epitomizes the free agent, embodying hegemonic assumptions of autonomy, although recent theories particularly in the field of STS studies (Latour, 2005) emphasize the innovative side of agency starting not so much from one's intentionality but rather from interactions with objects in the environment. These perspectives do not eliminate the dualism between structure and agency, amid which consumer is caught, but generally suggest that agency involves both acting and being acted upon. Therefore, processes of social change, resistance, or creativity are not solely attributable to individual intentional and subjective actions, nor are they merely the impersonal outcomes of a series of modifications. Instead, they emerge from a dynamic interplay of mutual and inextricable influences.

In contemporary society, consuming goods, and doing that in the most skillful way, has become a way of life. Consumerism is one of the main concepts around which the dualism between structure and agency revolves today. Consumerism may be defined as "a way of life common to the relatively rich societies, which promotes the continual purchase of consumer goods as beneficial for both the economy and personal ful-filment" (Giddens and Sutton, 2014), a way of life based on "lifestyles geared to possession and acquisition" (Lyon, 1994, p. 8).

As Gabriel and Lang (2006) show, consumerism in developed soci-eties evolved from a moral doctrine that served as the conduit for free-dom, power, and happiness, to an ideology of conspicuous consumption through which status and social distinction could be established. Later, it became an economic ideology for global development leading to ever higher standards of living in ever less regulated markets. Eventually it transformed into a political ideology that emphasizes unlimited con-sumption as a citizen's right to choose. In its latest form, consumerism evolved into a critical social movement that seeks to protect consumer rights, that criticizes unbridled consumption in a world of finite resourc-es, and advocates deconsumption and degrowth as an effect of the limits imposed by a fragile natural environment.

However, consumerism as an "active ideology that the meaning of life is to be found in buying things and pre-packaged experiences" (Bocock, 1993, p. 50) is still the undisputed core of our society, which is confronted with ecological change and whose guiding principle is not so much to consume less, even if frugality or waste avoidance are propagated, but to consume in a more environmentally friendly way. Consumption as a high-way to meet ordinary people's expectations of comfort and prosperity is what still makes it an ideology that aims to legitimize capitalist societies.

Despite the proclaimed call for a paradigm shift, the market continues to channel much of its efforts into ever more sophisticated strategies to capture even the slightest change in the contemporary disloyal and es-sentially unpredictable consumer, whom Gabriel and Lang (2006) refer to as "unmanageable."

In a world where everyone claims the consumer for her- or himself, the consumer must now be deemed unmanageable, claimed by many, but controlled by nobody, least of all by consumers themselves. The notion of unmanageability seems to us to be entirely appropriate for "an era where the capacity to plan must give way to opportunism, living for the present" (Gabriel and Lang, 2006, p. 194).

This uncontrollability, which according to the authors can be attribut-ed to the decline of the average mass consumer and the emergence of new forms of social inequality, has ushered in the post-Fordist era. An era marked by structural precarity, in which "fragmentation and contradictions" have emerged as key strategies for versatile adaptation and differentiation within contemporary consumption patterns (Gabriel and Lang, 2006, p. 4). Through a postmodernist lens, the decline of mass markets is viewed as offering unique opportunities for consumer choice. Each commodity is seen as a unique "sign" that can convey any meaning desired by advertisers or arbitrarily assigned by consumers themselves. This unprecedented ability to fragment into a myriad of signs or transform into various forms has resulted in consumers morphing, blending, or fragmenting (p. 24).

Following these introductory reflections about consumption and consumerism and taking inspiration from Gabriel and Lang's classification of the consumer as an actor become increasingly unmanageable, we can acknowledge some ideal typical features of consumers in contemporary consumeristic society based on their changeable relationship with consumer objects.

Before proceeding, it is crucial to establish a couple of premises. First, we would like to clarify that, unlike what Gabriel and Lang have suggested, the outlined unmanageable types do not represent many different and incommensurate models of the consumer. Taking into account the observation made by Warde (1997, p. 445), we believe that the different types are indeed indicative of the diversification of taste and approaches to consumption, which are distinctive but not incommensurable. In fact, the very fragmentation and unpredictability of the contemporary consumer make them more syncretic and contradictory than these distinctions, which are instead useful for analytical purposes.

Second, it is important to explain why this analysis refers to "ideal-types" rather than just "types" or "eco-types," as suggested by Huddart Kennedy (2022), especially in the context of growing ecological concerns in consumption. There are a few substantial reasons for this. First and foremost, it is because we maintain a focus on values in our sociological understanding of evolving consumer dynamics.

Indeed, in our sociological comprehension of the current shifts, we continue to view the social – including the market – as an analytical space where "a connection between individual and society is formed, making possible a conception of how social systems might be shaped by human will" (Coleman, 1986, p. 1310). However, this approach risks being seen as outdated due to its reference to rational action or structural individualism, particularly in light of neomaterialistic and neoontological perspectives. These perspectives aim to remove any subjective reference to the autonomous agent and to overcome the dualism of subject and object. They emphasize performers rather than agents, as figures engaged in carrying out socially shaped recursive patterns (Schatzki, 2002; Reckwitz, 2002a), or views where humans and nonhuman artifacts form a complex, inseparable, relational whole, acting and being enacted simultaneously (Latour, 2007).

Especially in the field of consumption, whether agency is approached as a cognitive impulse starting from the mind of a consumer opting for a vegetarian diet or cultured-cell-based alternatives for the sake of animal welfare, or as a relational evaluative situatedness involving decisions to abstain from farming-based products during ecological emergencies and to mitigate impending hardships, or as a performance embedded in social relations, routines, and constraints that shape consumer choices toward embracing specific dietary patterns, we still believe that without an agent there is no agency (Rebughini, 2023, p. 21).

Second, the notion of ideal types, instead of just types, highlights the attention to values that we reserve for our consumer analysis. Unlike Huddart Kennedy's intention to "disrupt the standard frameworks of values and behaviors" (Huddart Kennedy, 2022, p. 9) by substituting values with interests to facilitate practice-oriented "connections between subjects (people) and objects (a broad term encompassing people, ideas, consumer goods)," we argue that an analytical approach that considers values as a primary normative source guiding meaningful relationships within society – rather than external drivers – is essential for providing a sociological scope to the analysis of evolving consumer practices and behaviors. This is because, in the wake of the Weberian legacy that informs our analysis, we still believe that the recognition of social issues is inherently value-oriented and cannot disregard values. Nor can we abandon the essential trait of the cultural sciences – to which sociology of consumption belongs – of being disciplines that analyze the phenomena of life in terms of their cultural significance. As Weber states,

> Empirical reality becomes 'culture' to us because and insofar as we relate it to value ideas. It includes those segments and only those segments of reality which have become significant to us because of this value-relevance. (Weber, 2011, p. 76)

However pragmatically oriented one may be, value judgments informing cultural phenomena, such as consumption and its understanding, cannot be solely deduced from material interests, although they are not devoid of these interests, which should, on the contrary, be recognized and accounted for. Therefore, there is a need to understand shifting consumer trends in terms of ideal types, avoiding confining them to abstract configurations, but rather developing models to compare with concrete reality. This approach lends relevance and interpretative capacity beyond the specific and unique circumstances of the analysis, once again echoing the Weberian perspective, which I would like to refer to as follows:

> Only through ideal-typical concept-construction do the viewpoints with which we are concerned in individual cases become explicit. Their peculiar character is brought out by the confrontation of empirical reality with the ideal-type. (Weber, 2011, p. 110)

Based on these premises, we revisited Gabriel and Lang's (2006) identification of consumer types, endeavoring to encapsulate their proposed polymorphic typologies within a more schematic framework of ideal types. Our effort aimed to position a spectrum of potential relationships with market commodities along an ideal continuum, ranging from prevailing structural determinants to increasing individual agency (Figure 1).

While acknowledging the inherent oversimplification of this approach, we adhere to Weber's concept of the ideal type as an attempt to transform the empirical individual complexity into unified, one-sidedly emphasized but intelligible analytical constructs (Weber, 2011 [1922], p. 90). This spectrum of consumer types ranges from purely material entry into possession of an object (purchase or procurement) as a reactive search for satisfaction, strongly conditioned by structural constraints, to an increasingly symbolic appropriation of consumer goods with growing agency, understood as the capacity for choice, active selection, culminating in proactive forms of engagement and advocacy. These shifting consumer types take the shape of a "ladder" reflecting the core of the consumerist credo, which elevates individual choice to a supreme value. In the progressive elevation from "the dupe" to "the citizen," this image visualizes the consumerist representation of consumer status as a condition characterized by a growing scope of personal agency and a shrinking constraint by social structure on individual freedom and will.

Figure 1   Consumer ideal types in contemporary society

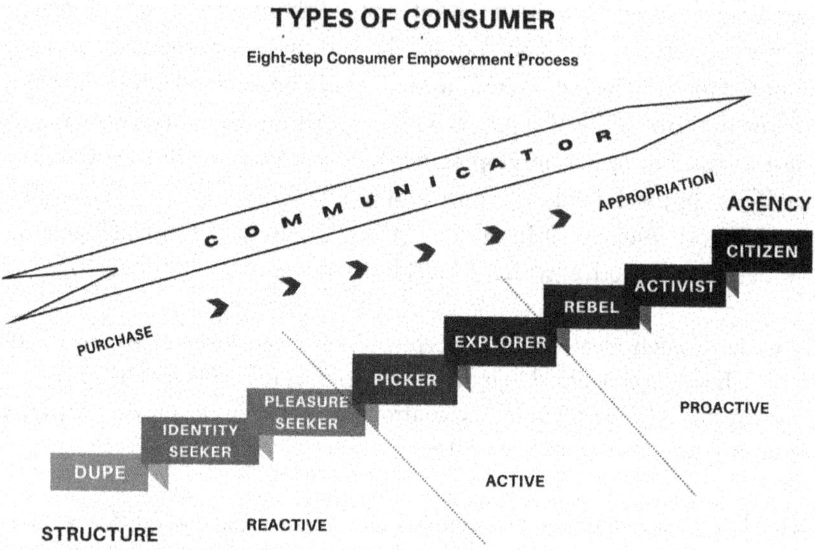

TYPES OF CONSUMER

Eight-step Consumer Empowerment Process

Source: Author's adaptation and revision of consumer classification proposed by Gabriel and Lang (2006).

From the bottom going upwards:

- *Consumer as a dupe*: The idea lying behind this characteristic is that consumers are a passive target of manipulative strategies employed by marketers and producers. They are portrayed as gullible, uncritical, or compulsive figures, crushed by structural constraints and at risk of being exploited as victims of social inequalities reproduction. This depiction reflects the type of consumer vulnerable to manipulation through mass advertising, as famously explored by Packard in his famous book *The Hidden Persuaders* (Packard, 1957).

- *Consumer as an "identity-seeker"* (Gabriel and Lang, 2006, p. 86): This is a typical figure of postmodernist society, where identity is meant as a lifelong self-aware fluid project, a potentially unstable and context-dependent one. While a flexible concept of identity is often presented as liberation from fixed categories and assigned status, the struggle for identity has become a main source for anxiety. As Giddens argues, identity lies now "in the capacity to keep a particular narrative going" (Giddens, 1991, p. 54). Therefore, consumers driven by a burgeoning desire for wholeness and authenticity through consumer objects are likely to exhibit strong brand loyalty, especially toward brands that position themselves as shelters. Within this consumer model but regarded from a critical perspective on consumer society, we find Baudrillard (1998) with his concept of consumption as sign manipulation induced by what he called "the strategists of desire" (Baudrillard, 1998, p. 35).

- *Consumer as a pleasure seeker*: This trait has to do with the hedonism typical of capitalistic and post-Fordist society. While traditional hedonism involved opulence, sumptuousness, and geared forms of "conspicuous," showy consumption, modern hedonism seeks pleasure less in sensations than in the emotions that accompany them – including apparently negative feelings such as sorrow, melancholy, and anger. The symbolic message conveyed by such a pleasure-based consumption is the expression of an identity that is less collectively and more individualistically organized.

- *Consumer as a picker*: Revisiting the concept of "chooser" proposed by Gabriel and Lang (2006, p. 25). If choosing is considered the primary skill of modern individuals, reflecting the qualities of Homo economicus – rational, efficient, and vigilant – then picking from an array of products, often by scrolling down a screen and purchasing with a simple click, epitomizes the skill of the contemporary consumer. On one side, there is the modern decision-maker whose discernment emphasizes accuracy in calculation, parsimony, and the ability to maximize utility. On the other side, there is the late-modern consumeristic posture of individuality, where purchasing becomes an exercise of free will, embodying personal uniqueness and lifestyle preferences amid a space saturated by the whimsical and changeable tastes of the insatiable consumer.

- *Consumer as an "explorer"* (Gabriel and Lang, 2006, p. 69): If the picker is driven by insatiable satisfaction, this type of consumer is driven by insatiable curiosity. Moving through the market with a more organized approach to memorable consumption than simply picking from a messy array, the explorer is on a quest for new experiences. The pursuit of experience becomes a central factor in consumption, a form of agency that demands discernment, partic-

ularly expressed through bargain-hunting and discovering hidden
treasures – an attitude distinctly different from simply demanding
value for money.

- *Consumer as a "rebel"* (Gabriel and Lang, 2006, p. 147): This figure
  expresses an even increasing agency in consumption and is represented by the rebellious consumer, who uses mass-market products
  subversively and iconoclastically. Rebellious consumption involves
  adopting acts of defiance against mainstream culture, which may
  manifest in reducing consumption, modifying consumption habits, or, in rare cases, abstaining from consumption altogether. They
  generally fight against commodification of consumer goods and ad-
  vocate for nonconformism to promote new lifestyles (consider the
  adjectives "rebel" or "unconventional" often associated with plant-
  based burgers). Consequently, if owning goods from mainstream
  culture symbolizes acceptance of established norms, individuals
  may prefer to identify with other types of goods that do not carry negative connotations. Rebellious consumption is rooted in this
  juxtaposition between acceptance and rejection, often taking on a
  moral dimension that leads to a dichotomy between "good" and
  "bad" goods (Gabriel and Lang, 2006, p. 135). However, sometimes the value of the unconventional is just an illusion of proac-
  tivity. Consumerism often seeks to assimilate and integrate these
  countercultural messages. In fact, it can be argued that all trends
  in consumption initially stem from resistance against consumer behaviors perceived as conformist and mainstream.
- *Consumer as an "activist"* (Gabriel and Lang, 2006, p. 170): Consumer activism is expressed through forms of commitment with
  values based both on group pressure and social movements that de-
  clare themselves champions of the consumer cause. Denunciation
  and boycotts are its fundamental tactics. Boycotts have long played
  a seminal role in consumer activism because they symbolize a rejection of the negative aspects of consumption and serve as acts of
  defiance by consumer activists. As stated by Gabriel and Lang (p.
  172), "They have 'bite', not just heart". Boycotts are not solely symbolic acts driven by good intentions, but they also exert substantial
  and tangible influence on their targets. They possess the ability to
  cause economic harm or damage a company's reputation, impacting
  individuals or countries at which they are aimed. As exemplified

in advertisements by movements like Green Peace, which openly blame a famous chocolate brand for causing deforestation with their productions, boycotts can lead to tangible outcomes and impacts instead of merely conveying disapproval or ethical positions.

- *Consumer as a "citizen"* (Gabriel and Lang, 2006, p. 193): This figure represents a higher, holistically conceived form of engagement and agency in society, where consumption is an ambit for exercising rights and responsibilities. Choosing as a citizen entails a very different evaluation of alternatives compared to choosing as a consumer. When citizens make choices, they are not as unbounded as the sovereign consumer who acts solely on their own behalf. Citizens bear a sense of superior responsibility; they must argue their views and engage with the perspectives of others (Gabriel and Lang, p. 174). The "bond" with others forms the core of the highest form of consumer engagement when they act as citizens, advocating common causes in the name of universalistic values (Falk, 1997, p. 103). This ideal type of consumer is often portrayed in advertisements advocating for humanity, justice, connection with nature, as well as with other living beings, and for getting rid of stereotypes, all while acting responsibly in the name of a supreme sense of good. While this equivalence between citizen and consumer may empower consumers to act as citizens through aware, responsible consumption, it also carries the risk of reducing citizenship to mere ownership in the market, where people are entitled to rights only as long as they can act as consumers of goods and services. In other words, the inclusive call for consumers to act as citizens risks becoming a marketing trap, excluding or blaming those who do not have the power to make the right choices. The emerging marketing frontier of branded entertainment, with its twofold emphasis on advocacy and product placement, serves as an example of this risk (Lehu, 2007).

Unlike Gabriel and Lang, and in line with Simmel, Veblen, Douglas, Baudrillard, Lash, and even Bourdieu, our perspective views consumers as communicators, irrespective of their ideal-typical consumer profile, demonstrating that they are different but not incommensurate. This is because their consumption choices are a form of communication that conveys information about themselves. The concept of communicating through consumption is essential for the sociological understanding of consumer behavior, where consuming extends beyond mere purchasing to the symbolic appropriation of goods. Through this act of appropriation, consumers convey symbolic messages primarily to others but also to themselves, often using goods as indicators of social status or assertions of personal distinctiveness.

1.5   Environmental limitations of consumeristic culture

This articulation of consumer types can be considered still valid as long as it is reviewed in the light of the rapid social changes that characterize the anthropocentric world economy of capitalism (Wallerstein, 1979). The phases of capitalism described above, characterized by the triumph and crisis of Fordism, the emergence of post-Fordism and globalization (largely as a result of neoliberal policies), the third industrial revolution centered on Internet Technology and biology, clear the way for a new, more-than-human, critical, and ecological era of the Anthropocene (Pellizzoni, 2022, p. 44).

Much of this socioeconomic transition depends on the extent to which the current phase of capitalism differs from earlier phases. For example, the recent fundamental reordering of political conflicts, in which the divide between left and right is becoming less important compared to the distribution of risks and gains of globalization (Azmanova, 2020), and the only recently revived polarization of the global order between East and West and the division of economic power among three blocks. But above all, the awareness that most of environmental degradation is owing to human behaviors, particularly the way we produce and consume.

Overall, it is estimated that food production is responsible for a quarter of global greenhouse gas emissions and that 21% of emissions come from the cultivation of crops intended for direct human consumption. About 18% of emissions are from supply chains where produce is processed from the farm into final products for consumption. This means that human food consumption accounts for between 20% and 40% of the total environmental impact (Ritchie, 2019). Unlike other consumer goods, food is a basic necessity that cannot be dispensed with or replaced. But developing an awareness of these consequences and adopting the right consumption habits within one's means can help change the game. Avoiding food waste does more to reduce emissions than eating locally sourced food (Gustavsson et al., 2013).

1.6 The contribution of sociology to the rise of consumer culture: Theories and approaches to understand consumption

Consumption is a multidisciplinary field that requires interdisciplinary collaboration for the purpose of strategic intervention (Warde, 2022, p. 12).

Sociology has provided a great contribution to consumption studies by providing a reading of consumer choices that go beyond the mere relationship between income and consumed goods. Of course, income affects the quantity and the quality of purchased foodstuffs, and economy is a value appealed to in many contexts in modern market societies. According to the economists' accounts, economizing should be the predominant consideration in exchange, but this value, together with utility maximization, is not enough to explain consumer choices and contrasting drives to economy and extravagance.

As a matter of fact, the best-established accounts of consumption are sociological, as sociology's main concern is the interest in the group differentiation arising from social norms and relationships rather than in that arising simply from money income.

Since its appearance at the beginning of the twentieth century, the sociology of consumer culture has started from the premise that consumption practices, in advanced capitalist societies, are themselves a clear reflection of class position.

One of the major contributions of the sociology of consumer culture has been to indicate the limits of approaches to consumption offered by neoclassical economics, which explains demand primarily as a simple relationship between the income of consumers, the price of goods, and a universal desire to maximize utility. Consumption decisions are directed by concern with the symbolic meanings of goods and indeed of different brands of goods performing identical practical functions, in addition to any consideration of cost (Warde, 1997, p. 97).

Class position is ineluctably associated with the unequal distribution of income and wealth and just because of this, it always provides some basis for different patterns of consumption behavior. Consumer culture connected social hierarchies to the display of commodities and engagement in activities that were attributed to different degrees of honor.

Moreover, consumer culture fosters the illusion that coveted items are universally available and accessible, while simultaneously promising purchasers the capacity, through proper choice, to render those items exclusive and thereby themselves superior to others. Such contradictory pretense is expressed by Hirsch's (1978) definition of "positional goods," or goods, services, and even work positions whose value depends on how many other people own them. Their characteristic is eminently symbolic, identifying the pursuit of exclusivity as a drive to adopt innovative and often fashionable practices which, as long as they remain exclusive, serve to enhance self-esteem and provide satisfaction. Once these practices are adopted by a large number of people, they become less attractive, because they no longer confer any special distinction.

Universal availability misses a key aspect of the logic of consumer society: *in order to function as a social marker of distinction, objects must be perceived as exclusive ones, because it is just this exclusiveness that makes them most appealing.*

It is the contribution of sociology that has legitimized taste as a sociological category in its own right, as well as its relevance to the sociology of consumption. Taste is intimately intertwined with markets, spaces, ideologies and, above all, identities, reflecting the contested and changing nature of culture. In fact, it is primarily the sociology of culture that emphasizes the aesthetic orientation toward food manifested in taste. Taste is what we refer to as an aesthetic orientation, namely, the ability to transform it into a judgement upon which we base our consumption decisions.

A generally accepted and shared definition of taste as a sociological category was provided by Bourdieu:

> Taste is an acquired disposition to 'differentiate' and 'appreciate' [...] to establish and mark differences by a process of distinction [...] (ensuring) recognition (in the ordinary sense). (Bourdieu, 1984, p. 466)

Taste becomes a distinguishing mark of exclusivity, a quality no longer peculiar to (positional) objects but to segments of the population, and it is the basis for the accumulation of cultural capital as a factor of social distinction. Theories of taste are often multidisciplinary, offering the possibility of expanding the field of analysis through cross-fertilization of concepts, ideas, and even research methods.

1.7   The methodological families within consumer studies

Halkier (2017) identifies four primary analytical "families" that are crucial for studying consumption in the social and cultural sciences. When conducting empirical research, it is essential to align methodological assumptions with the selected theoretical perspective.

What makes consumption a genuinely interdisciplinary area of study is the overlap of the following four features:

- The significance of broader contexts, such as economic, socioeconomic, and structural dynamics, which can significantly shape individual behaviors (consumption as behavior).
- The importance of smaller-scale contexts, encompassing communicative interpersonal dynamics through which individuals can articulate their identity (individuals primarily act as symbolic subjects).
- The relevance of intermediate-level contexts involving specific environments (formal, informal, and institutional) with which individuals interact as social actors and contribute to both subjective and objective formation (interaction between individuals and their surroundings).
- The significance of organized everyday settings including specific environments (formal, informal, and institutional) in which individuals partake in habitual socially organized activities, routines, that contribute to their continuity and to some extent change over time.

From a sociological perspective, consumption encompasses all four dimensions proposed by Halkier, which can be schematized as in Figure 2.

The four broad categories of consumer research around which research methods and discussions are organized follow Halkier's (2017) classification and can be described as follows:

Figure 2   The four analytical "families" considered as the primary groupings
for researching consumption

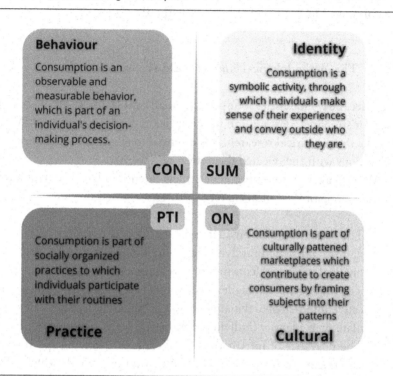

Source: Author's schematization and personal revisitation of the conceptualization proposed by Halkier (2017).

1. *Consumption as behavior*: This definition is usually emphasized in economic, psychological, and sociological disciplines, especially when applied to marketing. Consumption is seen as an observable and measurable behavior that is part of an individual's decision-making process. The *epistemological approach* is based on the positivist logic of discovery through systematic observation of manifest phenomena. Typically, *research questions* aim to understand the motives behind habitual patterns by asking questions such as "How important is this to you?" or "How likely are you to… use, buy, eat? The *unit of analysis* is the individual, with the focus on measurable behavioral patterns (habits), which are seen as phenomenal variations of basic invariant patterns and are therefore measurable and comparable. *The research ap-*

proach is quantitative and involves statistical modeling of self-reported behaviors, often in combination with direct observation when testing is the goal. Typical *research tools* include surveys, which are often supplemented by focus groups. The consumption as behavior research family includes theories such as Ajzen's Planned Behavior Theory (1985, 1991), Schwartz's Universal Human Values Theory (2006, 2012), and Grunert's Food-Related Lifestyles Theory (2005). These theories examine the motivational drivers and individual perceptions of food quality within a broader framework of lifestyle and culturally informed contexts. These theories, which emphasize consumer agency and choice, are often combined with each other (Grunert, 2007) or with Hofstede's indicators of cultural variability (Hofstede, 2001). Hofstede's theory is a monumental one, largely used in the context of marketing or organizational diversity management to understand, from a comparative and cross-cultural perspective, how different cultures function in different contexts.

2. *Consumption as an identity*: This definition is mainly used by disciplines such as cultural sociology, semiotics, communication studies, and social anthropology. Consumption is seen as a symbolic activity through which individuals give meaning to their experiences and communicate their identity to the outside world. In this case, this approach is relevant for marketing in order to identify consumer targets. The *epistemological approach* is based on narrative subjectivism and interpretative intersubjectivism, with communication and language playing a central role. The *research questions* generally aim to understand how consumers experience and make sense of their own and others' consumption. The *unit of analysis* is the symbolic/communicative individual who is intersubjectively embedded in a communicative context. The *research approach* is primarily qualitative, focusing on the discursive/narrative expression of consumers. However, it can also incorporate quantitative methods, particularly applied to textual analysis. Common *research tools* include individual narrative interviews, focus groups, and text analyses. In the field of consumption as identity, we encounter the influential theoretical work of Arnould and Thompson (2005), who have developed a specific brand of research called Consumer Culture Theory out of the sociocultural, experiential, symbolic, and ideological aspects that characterize consumer identity. In this area, we also consider theories such as Bauman's (2005, 2007), who emphasizes

contemporary consumption as an expression of the fragmentation of identity and commodification to which the subject is condemned in the postmodern era. In the cultural turn within food consumption studies, a prominent role is played by Mennell (1985), who, in his pioneering concept of "diminishing contrasts, increasing varieties" (1985, p. 319), highlights the ability of commodities, especially food, to erode social barriers and bridge longstanding gaps between individuals. Additionally, within this analytical family, we can also include Sassatelli (2019), who developed the concept of food consumer identity increasingly linked to authenticity and quality, as part of a cultural theory of consumer action.

3. *Consumption as a cultural dynamic*: This is the definition most frequently emphasized in disciplines such as cultural sociology, social psychology, and social anthropology of a constructivist matrix. Consumption is seen as part of culturally patterned marketplaces that contribute to the creation of consumers by embedding subjects in their patterns. The *epistemological approach* is rooted in social constructivism and critical realism. The *research questions* typically aim to understand market cultures, the sociohistorical structuring of consumption and the interplay between market discourses and consumer meaning-making. They ask questions such as: "What is the cultural context of consumption?," "How are the subject positions of consumers discursively generated?," and "How have certain consumption patterns developed historically? The *unit of analysis* is intersubjectively produced cultural patterns, based on the interaction between communicative subjects and cultural contexts. The *research approach* is predominantly qualitative, namely, ethnographic situationism and semiotic interactionism. Common *research tools* include nonintrusive participant observation, active interviewing, and text/discourse analysis, reported through qualitative surveys. In particular, active interviewing (Holstein and Gubrium, 1995) is a social constructivist type of interview that is understood as a nonneutral process, assuming that all participants (including the interviewer) act socially and create cultural meanings. Active interviewing includes, for example, the use of materials and texts that encourage interaction and, in the case of consumption topics, reveal the ambivalent brand framing of consumer choices – which simultaneously shapes and empowers them – thus contributing to a shift in cultural positions. In this analytical family, we might include interaction-oriented perspectives, where interaction is less conceived

in terms of increasing individual motivation to adopt desirable behaviors, as seen in nudging strategies incorporated into our appliances or smartphones to embrace more healthy dietary styles (Thaler and Sunstein, 2021), and more as the use of platforms that ask users to share their feedback about consumer objects in a common interactive space, which may take the form of a community. In this space, users comment on and are commented upon regarding their mutual consumer experiences, creating a common practical-evaluative framework that loops back to reconsider both the objects and the subjects involved in this interaction, and the relationship between them (Maffesoli, 1996 [1988], 2016).

4. *Consumption as a component of social configurations*: This definition is mainly emphasized in disciplines such as sociology, with moderate consideration of sociocultural approaches. In this definition, consumption is seen as part of socially organized practices in which individuals actively participate and which they reproduce through their routines. The *epistemological approach* is grounded in practice theory advocating an anti-individualistic perspective with a focus on inconspicuous forms of consumption. The approach is characterized by the diminishing role of the acting subject in favor of the organization of the activities being performed. The *research questions* typically aim to understand the temporal and spatial organization of everyday, often unreflected activities and how these are normalized and integrated into routines. They ask questions such as: "How is the context of certain types of consumption organized socially and spatially?," "How are consumption patterns scheduled?," "How are object uses embodied in routines?," "How do individuals participate in routines?," and "How are consumption patterns reproduced and transformed socially, spatially and materially?" The *unit of analysis* is social practice, which encompasses routine activities as part of social configurations that include organized settings with other people, focusing not on agents but on the actions and their objects. In the field of consumer research, practice-theoretical research adheres to what could be termed "non-consumption-centric" consumption research, insofar as the analytical unit is usually neither consumers nor consumption, but the socially, materially and spatially organized contexts of these two (Halkier, 2017, p. 42). The *research approach* is predominantly qualitative, especially ethnographic, although quantitative analyses such as structural data and digital tracking are also employed. Typical *research tools* in-

clude participant observation, qualitative interviews as well as quantitative surveys, time-use analyses (especially to capture social change) and digital data.

The practice approach is grounded in Schatzki's definition of practice as "the locus of the social" (2002) and his assertion that practice theory undermines the traditional individual/nonindividual divide by appropriating, in transfigured form, a variety of individualist explanations while grounding them in a supra-individual phenomenon (Schatzki, 2001, p. 5). According to Schatzki's perspective on practice theory, individual behavior cannot be seen as an explanation for structures, just as it cannot be assumed that structures are capable of explaining individual behavior. This argument is still close to Giddens' notion of the inseparable duality of agency and structure, keeping practice theory in a middle position between approaches that emphasize agency and choice (and the values that sustain them) and those that emphasize socially shaped blocks of action as preexistent and informing individual behavior, which individuals "fill out," mostly unreflectively, as mere bearers of socially organized patterns of performance (Reckwitz, 2002a, p. 250). Practice theory would later evolve into stronger formulations, dismissing subjective agency as a "nonsociological" object of study (Evans, 2019, p. 499). Shove (2010) provides examples of these approaches, illustrating the "incommensurability" between contrasting paradigms, and advocating for a departure from the "ABC" paradigm, where "A" stands for attitude, "B" for behavior, and "C" for choice when addressing challenges posed by structural phenomena like climate change (Shove, 2010, p. 1279). A more recent formulation moving in the direction of a strong theory of practice is provided by Huddart Kennedy (2022), who proposes an understanding of the environment in people's lives and outlines eco-social relationships as eco-type configurations. In her explanatory pathway, the practice-theoretical stance relies on the rejection of values as objects of study, considering them nonrelational categories, and replacing them with "interests," regarded as more immediately practical stances dynamically embedded within socially configured relationships (Huddart Kennedy, 2022, p. 9). She emphasizes the risks of "motivational approaches" leading to biased idealizations of human actions and appeals to American sociological pragmatism, for example, Wright Mills, to ground her positioning, presenting her value-skipping approach as a fact. This is quite far from the Weberian lesson of a value-free stance as a qualifying trait of sociological understanding, to which even Bourdieu, the father of practice theory, adheres (Bourdieu, 1984, p. xii) and extends by reconceptualizing status as an integral part of class-namely, the symbolic, value-based side of class privileges. Dismissing values in favor of interests sounds like shifting the focus of sociological imagination from what Weber called "value-rational action" (*wertrational*) to the narrow means-end orientation of "instrumentally rational action" (*zweckrational*) (Weber, 2012, p. 501), giving up, in the name of practice, the power of "valuation" (*Wertung*) as the ultimate generator of social relevance and normative boundaries within human actions (Weber, 2012, p. 499). Although practice theory continues to reject any focus on individual choice as necessitating "individualistic explanations" (Warde, 2014, p. 283) and presents itself as an alternative to "the cultural turn" and its emphasis on "webs of cultural meanings which constitute symbolic resources for individual choice" (Warde, 2014, p. 279), it has nevertheless confronted the risk of "militating away" from the use of concepts and categories that may capture general understanding that inform practices (Welch, 2020, p. 63). Terms like "teleoaffective formations" have been coined to address, in an operational way, large-scale configurations of discourse inhabiting practices (Welch and Warde, 2017; Welch, 2020). Additionally, authors like Spaargaren et al. (2006) have highlighted that, in times of transition, the role of human agency must be systematically considered. They depict citizens/consumers as "knowledgeable and capable actors" (2006, p. 109), not simply bearers of performances but also agents of change who make transitions possible (2006, p. 118).

Although theoretical discernment is part of academic speculations, and the lay consumer is far removed from these distinctions, awareness of the distinctive factors of these analytical families is crucial for scholars and stakeholders. This awareness is essential when deciding how to address a social issue arising in the market involving consumption, how to formulate research questions that delve into the effects of those issues on consumer life, and which methods and techniques are most suitable to appropriately inquire into those questions and test hypotheses to sketch possible solutions.

Part II
What Do We Eat Today?
Old and New Eating Dilemmas
in Times of Crisis

2 Plant-Based Proteins or Cheeseburger? Exploring Opposing Food Consumer Predicaments

2.1 Revisiting taste antinomies in current foodscapes

When we enter a grocery store or supermarket, we are faced with choices that present themselves as dilemmas: Should I take a chance and try something new, or should I opt for familiar options? In these difficult times, will I be more likely to save a euro on grated cheese that bears the brand of the supermarket chain where I am shopping, or will I prefer to rely on that famous brand that costs a little more but is familiar to me (reminding me of who I am)?

In 1997, Alan Warde, one of the most influential scholars in the study of food consumption, who in his practice theoretical approach always accounted for cultural understanding, identified four conflicting patterns of taste antinomies gripping consumers. Drawing on Kantian philosophy, he termed these dilemmas "antinomies," symbolizing humanity's endeavor to apply rational thought to practical reasoning in order to reconcile equally rational yet contradictory outcomes in practice.

These dilemmas can be regarded as indicators of deep-seated cultural understandings, as they provide a systematic basis for comprehending the underlying reasons behind consumer choices. They also represent the complex intersection of contradictory messages through which food is understood, represented, and recommended for purchase. Warde intended the antinomies of taste as "permanent features of the modern predicament" (Warde, 1997, p. 56), wherein competence lies in the ability to decide between alternative courses of action in the sphere of consumption.

Warde intended the antinomies of taste as "permanent features of the modern predicament" (Warde, 1997, p. 56), wherein competence lies in the ability to decide between alternative courses of action in the sphere of consumption. In this definition, taste antinomies are not simply indicators of typical consumer interests, as in the wake of recent practical-theoretical approaches to consumer types (Huddart Kennedy, 2022). Instead, at least in our reading, they seem to be closer to Weber's ideal types, functioning not as normative ideals but rather as heuristic instruments or models used to frame reality, which could easily have been given a corresponding name (Weber, 2012, p. XXIV).

Warde's four antinomies are: novelty *vs.* tradition; health *vs.* indulgence; economy *vs.* extravagance; and care *vs.* convenience (1997). We revisit them twenty-seven years later, in an updated reading for our times, and also try to envision their evolution into new dilemmas during times of transition.

These taste antinomies can serve as a framework for understanding the ultimate values that drive consumers to prioritize certain characteristics in their choices. They also help identify the alignment between these values and the brand strategies employed in product description, valuation, and recommendation. Taste antinomies cater to both consumer and marketer perspectives, offering valuable analytical insights into delineating the cultural attributes of a market within a social context or country. Far from simply being descriptive categories of consumer objects, these antinomies embody underlying values that are culturally fixed and, in most cases, operate beneath the threshold of consumer consciousness. They serve to legitimize the choice among foodstuffs.

As they represent opposite poles of attraction when making purchases, these antinomies frame the central dilemmas of contemporary consumerism and experience, often causing anxiety. They can be viewed as the crystallization in common consciousness of individuals' central dilemma: Making the best choice among an increasing number of alternative options.

The four antinomies integrate the main structure/agency dualism that shapes the patterns of consumption and all behavior in social life. According to Warde, these antinomies reflect the structural concerns of our time, establishing boundaries of uncertainty that often impact consumers' decisions and create feelings of guilt and discomfort. This becomes particularly evident when we consider Warde's observation that they mirror the key concepts of modern culture: Individuality, corporeality, money, and time (1997, p. 56). From the time when Warde wrote his book in the late nineties to the present day, we observe that these antinomies have evolved into new dilemmas, such as the tension between safe and risky, local and global, high and low environmental footprint, fake and authentic, and ethical and unethical. These concerns characterize the contemporary consumer and also represent some of the fundamental factors driving what Pollan referred to as "the omnivore's dilemma":

> To one degree or another, the question of what to have for dinner assails every omnivore, and always has. When you can eat just about anything nature has to offer, deciding what you should eat will inevitably stir anxiety, especially when some of the potential foods on offer are liable to sicken or kill you. This is the omnivore's dilemma (Pollan, 2006, p. 3).

These antinomies delineate the central dilemmas of contemporary consumer consciousness and experience, embodying fundamental options that are increasingly viewed as irreducible and irreconcilable oppositions in consumer choices within the polarizing culture in which we reside, a culture that constantly urges individuals to take a stance through their consumer behavior.

2.1.1 *Novelty versus Tradition revisited*

This antinomy (Warde, 1997, pp. 57-77) brings us into the realm of identity, where the pull of ingroup drives, advocating conformism, and the push of outgroup factors, advocating change, influence the process of identity formation, which also occurs through consumption. Novelty *vs.* tradition reflects the cultural category of individuality, oscillating between neophilic and neophobic tensions. This antinomy evokes a paradoxical condition described by the French sociologist Claude Fischler as specifically pertaining to omnivores:

> On the one hand, needing variety, the omnivore is inclined towards diversification, innovation, exploration and change, which can be vital to its survival; but on the other hand, it has to be careful, mistrustful, 'conservative' in its eating: any new, unknown food is a potential danger. (Fischler, 1988, p. 276)

The omnivore's paradox embodies the inherent tension between two opposing forces: Neophobia, characterized by prudence, fear of the unknown, and resistance to change, and neophilia, which represents the inclination to explore, the craving for novelty, and the pursuit of variety. As omnivores, the act of incorporation holds profound significance for us. Due to the principle of incorporation, the identification of food becomes a central element in shaping our identity. Moreover, acknowledging the vital and symbolic importance of identity and identification, humans have ingeniously crafted cuisine, where this primordial dynamic is ceaselessly in motion.

2.1.1.1 Novelty as smart dietary updates

In a consumeristic society, finding pleasure through the consumption of new items has emerged as the primary source of enjoyment (Baudrillard, 1988, p. 48). Conversely, feeling pleasure through the acquisition of new items has transformed into an obligation and the very motivation for consumption. The pursuit of new pleasures is no longer solely the responsibility of consumers but has become a societal obligation. This universal curiosity, coupled with staying informed about all the latest developments in the market, reignites curiosity across various domains including cuisine, culture, science, religion, sexuality, and more. Consumeristic society is pervaded by the cultivation of novelty, which embodies the spirit of restlessness and the associated pursuit of fashion. As highlighted by Warde (1997, p. 56), in the seventies, the Christian gospel song saying "Try Jesus!" became a slogan, suggesting that faith itself could become an object of novelty, discovery, and consumption, meaning that everything, including religion, should be "tried" and experienced as if it were the first time. As evidenced by the myriad of religious content websites proliferating on the internet and social media, often labeled as "Religion 2.0" or "Faith 2.0," everything, whether old, or new, is likely to become the object of user reviews once it becomes digital content. "New" is one of the main characteristics encapsulated by the word "smart," which conveys both innovation and intelligence. This trend particularly affects food, whose enormous success on social media relies on the personal reinterpretation of traditional preparations. Additionally, alternative, for example, "novel" dietary styles such as ethical veganism may take on the characteristics of a religion for their adherents

(Johnson, 2015). The constant development of new products and the endless creation of new desires on the part of consumers are the essential mechanisms for the reproduction of modern capitalism and its consumer culture. The requirement for continuous innovation among producers is well recognized, but the core principle of digital communication systems is the process of engaging and persuading consumers that they desire more and new items, constantly alerting us to what's new.

There are different ways to present novelty in consumption: New, exotic, out-of-the-ordinary – especially if it is juxtaposed with the routine of daily life – adventurous, experimental, and innovative. These various meanings of the word "new" regularly appear in social media updates, advertisements, and dedicated websites, often in the form of nudges, alerts, notifications, and so on. These innovations are rarely associated with words suggesting unfamiliarity, especially in the realms of food, as they might appear unusual or suspicious, but are instead presented as part of our smartness. If an item or activity is presented as "new," its appeal increases. Thus, in food advertisements, novelty serves as a constant basis of appeal: Newness is a property that promises excitement, adventure for individuals, and progress at the institutional and personal level. However, constant innovation and perpetual change can cause social uncertainty and personal disruptions, which Fischler terms "gastro-anomie" (1977), as well as anxiety about making the right choice, which Pollan (2006) calls the "omnivore's dilemma."

2.1.1.2 Tradition as resistance to "novel food"

Opposite to novelty is the idea of tradition. Tradition embodies the sense of the familiar, reassurance, and the neophobic tensions of identity. The expression "the invention of tradition" was coined by Hobsbawm and Ranger (1983) to describe a social process whereby new activities or objects are given legitimacy by the pretense that they are timeless. Such inventions are integral parts of modernity, avoiding the risk that the idea of suspicious unfamiliar permeates new items of consumption. Over the last thirty years, the tourist industry has busily worked at such a revival of tradition, by providing impressions of regional and local customary feature of activities and products promoted to attract visitors. Local food habits or specialities played a role in such a re-creation or invention of spectacular events, rituals or practices evoking endless traditions.

In the gastronomic field, a dish is particularly appealing when it successfully combines the two poles of novelty and culinary tradition, thereby restoring a sense of complete identity. This is one of the main functions of cuisine in the common imagination and one of the reasons why renowned chefs often focus on revisiting traditional dishes rather than inventing new ones from scratch. But it is also one of the reasons why the binomial "tradition and innovation" has become a mantra of gastronomic tourism and brand marketing. Fischler had already anticipated this trend by far in the 1980s:

> It sets all these things in the order of the world and so confirms that the world is still in order. A cuisine enables neophile innovation to be reconciled with neophobic 'conservatism' or distrust. Novelty, the unknown, can be steeped in the sauce of tradition; originality is tempered by familiarity and monotony relieved by variety. (Fischler, 1988, p. 291)

As suggested by Warde (1997, p. 64), the word "tradition" in the realm of food practices takes on four main distinct senses: *Customary*, that is, conforming to the national cuisine, familiar to all audience members, customers, or members of a country or community; *Long-lived*, that is, old-fashioned but still valuable preparations that combine nostalgia and demand action (consumption) to rescue them from obscurity or extinction; *Creatively re-adaptable*, that is, suitable to be revised by improvisation on tradition; and *Genuine*, that is, conveying the idea of authentically reflecting a particular culinary ways of preparing food. Some cuisines, such as Italian cuisine, are strongly evocative of this sense of tradition.

This is also the reason why tradition is gradually detaching itself from the concept of "typical," perceived as "fake," and is becoming more closely associated with the concept of authenticity.

In recent times, the connection between tradition and authenticity has become a prevailing trait in consumer choices, driven by an increasing quest for pure identity on the one side and integrity on the other. As part of a widespread ideal of integrity, authenticity has become a value-laden concept that is not only descriptive of a diet or lifestyle but also part of a philosophy of living with a strong moral value. Being so immediately bound to identity, the novelty-tradition antinomy lends itself to a political appropriation of culinary discourses, resulting in the easy polarization of discussions.

Let's consider the recent discussions at both the national and supranational levels regarding the introduction of the so-called "novel food," including both alternative protein-based food and (by now, researched) cultivated meat as a substitute for conventional farming-based meat.

Periodically, regulations are issued authorizing the introduction of new foods to the market. In the European context, Regulation (EU) 2015/2283 of the European Parliament and of the Council of November 25, 2015 revised the definition and categories of foods that constitute novel foods, updating Regulation (EC) No. 258/97, in light of the scientific and technological developments since 1997. As we read in Article 8 of the Regulation text, the new categories of novel food are defined as follows:

> [...] Those categories should cover whole insects and their parts. There should be, inter alia, categories for food with a new or intentionally modified molecular structure, as well as for food from cell culture or tissue culture derived from animals, plants, microorganisms, fungi or algae, for food from microorganisms, fungi or algae and for food from material of mineral origin. There should also be a category covering food from plants obtained by non-traditional propagating practices where those practices give rise to significant changes in the composition or structure of the food affecting its nutritional value, metabolism or level of undesirable substances. The definition of novel food may also cover food consisting of certain micelles or liposomes. (Regulation (EU) 2015/2283)

From that moment on, new species have been included in the special category of insect-based novel food, such as the migratory locust, the domestic cricket, the flour moth, grasshoppers, mealworms, but also plant-derived proteins, such as mung bean protein. All of them have been introduced because they are considered safe following a positive opinion from EFSA, the commission of nutrition expert scientists of the EU. Factors like climate change and shifting consumer preferences toward healthier and more sustainable diets, including reduced meat consumption, underscore the necessity of systematically introducing new food sources and production systems to bolster food security. Novel foods are crucial for enhancing food security and resilience amid resource scarcity challenges, diversifying food sources, and offering sustainable production alternatives. Additionally, they can aid in waste reduction, resource optimization, and mitigating global hunger and food shortages.

This awareness has led the FAO (2022) to recommend to different countries around the world to have a forward-thinking and favorable view not only toward the introduction of already known food sources, such as edible insects, jellyfish, and algae, but also toward the production of foods based on lab-grown cells, highlighting the need for these to be subject to study, scientific research, and technological innovation to ensure their safety for human health. But when the novel food regulation, particularly concerning new meat alternatives, touches on the topic of cultivated meat or "cell-cultured meat" originating from a few cells obtained from living animals and then grown under controlled conditions in bioreactors, the discourse easily lends itself to polarization under the antinomy novel/tradition, where novel means dangerous and tradition means safe. Such associations in meaning, intrinsic to the taste antinomy, are also easily exploited by political discourse, specifically political marketing geared toward easy consensus grabbing, which prefers simple polarization between new/old, familiar/unfamiliar, dangerous/safe over in-depth arguments.

These discourses flattened on the identity antinomy of novelty/tradition become daily bread for the nationalist winds blowing especially in Europe, also because they leverage the economic interests of producers and breeders. For this reason, within the EU, the debate has heated up, and the EU has not yet taken a clear stance on the matter, loosening the process of innovation and sustainability of the European food system.

In the EU, there are still prejudices against cultivated meat, as evidenced by a recent note[1] presented by Austria, France, and Italy and supported by the Czech, Cypriot, Greek, Hungarian, Luxembourgish, Maltese, Polish, Romanian, Slovak, and Spanish delegations. The note requests the EU to conduct further investigations before the approval of these products. The document invokes various arguments, foremost among them safeguarding high-quality and primary farm-based food production, which is immediately defined as guarantors of food security juxtaposed with the European project of innovation and sustainability in the food system, which automatically falls into the opposite antinomy pole of risk and food insecurity.

---

[1] The note can found at the following link: https://data.consilium.europa.eu/doc/document/ST-5469-2024-INIT/en/pdf (accessed on 01/07/2024).

Italy has already issued a ban[2] on the production and marketing of cultivated meat in order to "protect the interests of health and cultural heritage." Other countries, such as Denmark and the Netherlands, have spoken out against the ban. The Netherlands is a pioneer in the development of cultured meat in the EU. Dutch companies can now submit their dossiers to apply for authorization to carry out tastings under controlled conditions before their products are approved.

Since there is not yet clear European regulation on the specific topic of cultivated meat, Italian law serves only a preventive function, in protection according to the precautionary principle. Put differently, until the EU authorizes the first food product based on cultivated meat, the law will retain a more propagandistic than substantial value.

Meanwhile, the antinomy of novel/harmful *vs.* traditional/safe has taken over the public sphere, polarizing discourse between conservative parties (e.g., sovereigntist, anti-EU sustainable policies parties) and progressive political parties (e.g., progressive pro-EU sustainable policies parties). This polarization is also fueling protests by farmers, whose interest would be affected by the advent of cell-based cultured meat production. The discourse touches on other new and old taste antinomies, such as health *vs.* indulgence.

2.1.2 *Health versus Indulgence revisited*

The tension between health and indulgence (Warde, 1997, pp. 78–97) also arises from the paradox inherent in the omnivore's principle of incorporation, where the body serves as the boundary between a safe interior and a dangerous exterior. In this context, consumer "sovereignty" doesn't align with either side of the antinomy. Instead, consumerist society celebrates the ability of consumers to alternate between these two dimensions, demonstrating a strategic capability to move in and out of self-control. This attitude is less about moderation and more about the market's need for consumers to experience a broader range of sensations, thereby enhancing their propensity to consume. In fact, the antinomy hints at the contradictory messages coming from our late-modern capitalistic society,

---

[2] Law n. 172/2023, the text is available at the following link: https://www.gazzettaufficiale.it/eli/id/2023/12/01/23G00188/sg (accessed on 01/07/2024).

which promotes both hedonistic pleasure and responsible self-restraint. We are encouraged to eat healthily, but not if it makes us unhappy.

An implicitly consumeristic and ultimately hedonistic message justifies adhering to both of these contrasting patterns of consumption by invoking two psychological attitudes toward food, expressed through the juxtaposition of what the mind and body need. This apparent dilemma between mental indulgence and bodily self-discipline can only be resolved by choosing to eat something different tomorrow. Ultimately, the message remains entirely self-centered and self-directed: eat with an eye on your health, but also keep in mind that "healthy" doesn't always align with what your mind and body need to be happy.

Hence the increasing need for the proliferation of alternative choices, between healthy and comfort food in late-modern societies. Rather than responding to rigid diet plans, both lunch and dinner have become extremely flexible, allowing eaters to choose what combination of foods to eat. Lists of many alternative treats have come to be included in the food magazines, food websites, and dietary books, with a calorie count for each dish or suggested eating pattern.

This is one of the reasons why veganism has also taken the shape of a lifestyle rather than just a way of life. Scholars such as Giraud (2021) use the term "lifestyle veganism" to encompass meat-free diets as a possibility, a result of the so-called "plant-based capitalism," a food system that, while promoting a healthier and more mindful lifestyle, does not relinquish catering to the capitalistic imperative of individual choices, nor engage in relevant advocacy for interspecies social justice (Giraud, 2021, pp. 129–131). The proliferation of vegan and vegetarian online communities, often reviewing eating experiences in plant-based restaurants, fuels this dual process of promoting unconventional practices as alternative value patterns while also mainstreaming them.

2.1.2.1 Health as a taste for sustainable eating

Healthy food is a concept that entered the common awareness and representation of food by the start of the eighties. During the sixties and the seventies, healthiness was not a main issue and even the appeal to the functional aspects of nutrition was rare and occasionally related to children's food. Association of food intake with the anxieties around health risks escalated some time thereafter, so as to give rise to a "language of health" in food discourses rich in factual information about fat, fibers, calories, etc. Such a health-conscious language came to permeate routine cookery articles and discourse, becoming the main feature of nineties. Alan Warde (1997, p. 84) presents examples from a well-known woman's magazines with inserts on cookery from the early 1990s, Prima, featuring titles such as "Finding your way through the vitamin maze" (Prima, Nov 1991), "Minerals – a down-to-earth guide" (Prima, Aug 1992), and "Are you throwing vitamins down the drain?" (Prima, May 1992), with the language reaching its climax in an article opening with the phrase "In the health-conscious nineties." During that period, the language utilized in specialized food magazines also started praising the benefits of healthy eating for medical issues, emphasizing the importance of specialized dietary plans, such as, for example, in response to cancer. Over time, the concept of "healthy" has been enriched with new consumer concerns. Healthy is no longer associated only with aesthetic or fitness concerns, focusing primarily on nutritional facts. Instead, it is increasingly associated with potential harmful effects on oneself, the community, animal welfare, and the planet. The growing attention to characteristics such as cleanliness, being GMO-free, and being organic is a prominent feature of the 2000s. Let's think at the well-known manifesto-book "Good, clean, and fair" by Petrini (2005). Additionally, by the end of the 1990s, the EU began regulating the introduction of new foods with a focus on public and consumer health protection. This included implementing labeling policies to ensure adequate and accurate information, particularly regarding GMO foods, with initial references to their potential damage to the environment adding to existing information about damage to consumers (see Regulation (EC) No. 258/97).[3] Particularly with the pandemic outbreak, healthy food has become top concern for both consumers, and producers as well as for policymakers. Healthy and sustainable diets have become part of a resilience process, as stated in the "Farm to Fork" strategy published by the European Commission in 2020, in the aftermath of the pandemic outbreak, where informing and incentivizing people about healthy and sustainable food choices is presented as part of consumer empowerment (European Commission, 2020, p. 14).

---

[3] The text of the Regulation (EC) No. 258/97 is available at the following link: https://eur-lex.europa.eu/legal-content/EN/TXT/?uri=CELEX:31997R0258 (accessed on 01/07/2024).

As discussed earlier in reference to the novel/traditional antinomy, healthy foods, including novel formulations categorized as novel foods, and the latter also including superfoods, are proving to be relevant in today's world, particularly as they address health concerns. These foods have the capability to meet the evolving needs and desires of consumers in the contemporary consumption paradigm. Their relevance lies in their ability to cater to changing consumer tastes, which are increasingly oriented toward healthy eating, particularly through reducing red meat consumption or adopting flexitarian diets, but without making sacrifices. Additionally, they promote overall health and wellness, address sustainability concerns, leverage technological advances, acknowledge cultural diversity, and contribute to food security and resilience – all requirements depicting the profile of today's skillful consumer.

The emphasis on staying fit as a pathway to good health hasn't been solely a prerogative of the 1990s. On the contrary, the advent of the internet, the rise of social media, and, above all, mobile apps have favored the proliferation of devices offering solutions for healthy lifestyles without giving up the pleasures of life. Technology has promoted the widespread use of nudges embedded in the digital devices that accompany us daily, turning them into an elective strategy to guide consumer behaviors toward socially and personally desirable choices (Thaler and Sustein, 2021). Our smartphones are full of nudges, from default display and ringtone solutions, to the free download meal planners, calorie counters, step trackers, and other apps promising rapid and customized results without making sacrifices. According to the definition provided by Thaler and Sustein, a nudge is

> any aspect of the choice architecture that alters people's behavior in a predictable way without forbidding any options or significantly changing their economic incentives. To count as a mere nudge, the intervention must be easy and cheap to avoid. (Thaler and Sustein, 2021, p. 7)

Who among us, upon their, has never received an invitation to download an app where a personal AI assistant promises to make us healthy and slim in fifteen days? Or who has never given a "like" to, or doesn't follow, an influencer who offers plant-based recipes or delicious gluten-free, lactose-free meals suitable for people with special dietary needs? Nudges have definitely transformed consumption within the sphere of "libertarian paternalism," the "paternalism of means, not of ends," where, in a game of agency acting and being acted upon, architects of choices (governments, policymakers, marketers, etc.) try to influence people's behaviors toward legitimate choices – in this case, healthier and better lifestyles – but in a way that makes "choosers better off, as judged by choosers themselves" (Thaler and Sunstein, 2021, p. 6).

Figure 1   Examples of meal planner apps nudging users toward healthier dietary styles

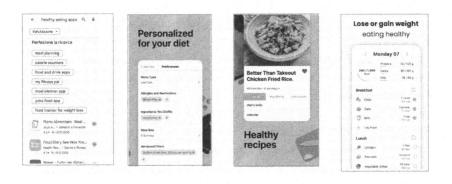

The era of mobile digital technology has exponentially amplified the call to stay healthy, through devices ranging from simple step counters installed in smartphones, to home fitness apps, to apps combining fitness and nutrition, aimed at preventing the development of metabolic diseases (Figure 1). AI is already at work and will further contribute to the increasingly accurate profiling of individuals, leading us toward a new frontier of medicine primarily focused on prevention. Another new frontier gaining attention in the social and health sciences is gamification. As a strategy integrated into this human/machine interaction, gamification aims to shape people's daily routines and lifestyles by introducing challenges, nudges, milestones, and rewards – elements of gaming – into the recommended desired behaviors (Lupton, 2020; Schmidt-Kraepelin et al., 2020; Cotton and Patel, 2019; King et al., 2013). Health emerges as a prominent dimension in the dilemmas confronting contemporary consumers. Opposite to this trend is comfort food, an indulgent solution when feeling blue, representing another significant aspect of self-care in today's world.

2.1.2.2 Indulgence as calculated decontrol

The motto summarizing the call to be an indulgent consumer is, "You deserve to be happy, and to be comforted when not." Comfort food epitomizes the indulgence pole of this antinomy. In Warde's words, comfort food is "the food you eat when your heart is broken, your boss is being impossible" (Warde, 1997, p. 78). Emphasis on feeling or an emotional approach to consumer objects is typically associated with the appeal to be indulgent in food intake, which is also a push toward intensive consumption or manipulative intentions by marketers.

The typical appeal to indulgence relies on encouraging people to try novelties in highly emotional situations, such as stressful work, socializing with friends or at a party, or dining out. Examples include the famous chocolate bar KitKat, renowned worldwide for its motto "take a break," accompanied by the sound of the bar breaking in half. But let's consider the advertisements for the famous Pringles® potato chips, which since the 1980s have focused not only on the indulgence of different flavors but also on compulsive, excessive, irrational consumption, accompanied by the sound of crispiness, as a response to a kind of chips-craving. Typically, advertisements for sweets, chocolate, potato chips, and ice cream use strong sensory stimuli aimed at eliciting responses that are both irrational and indulgent. If we believe this to be part of an old brand communication, we are mistaken, because comfort food advertisements, whether aired or screened on the web, always appeal to emotions that trigger strong and uncontrollable responses, namely, the indulgence of the consumer. In a chips advertisement aired on December 30, 2019, by the popular brand Cheez-It® Snap'd®, scientists in a taste-testing laboratory are depicted losing control and experiencing an overwhelming frenzy over a new type of thin, crispy, and cheesy chips.[4] Another typical situation evoked by comfort food is being with others or eating out, as for most people, eating out represents an emblematic circumstance for being indulgent with food. Indeed, eating out is a convivial situation where rules about healthy eating are suspended, and yielding to temptations is allowed. (Warde and Martens, 1995).

This antinomy between health and indulgence is widely diffused, especially throughout the middle class, representing the skills required of the

---

[4] The spot is available at the following link: https://www.ispot.tv/ad/ZKi4/cheez-it-snapd-taste-test (accessed on 15/07/2024).

contemporary consumer. According to Bourdieu's theory of distinction, the middle classes generally share this somewhat inconsistent combination of indulgence and self-discipline in their eating and drinking behaviors. In emulative Western societies, where success means achieving the material conditions and lifestyles of the immediately upper class fractions on the social ladder, the middle classes are characterized by groups whose lifestyle combines the self-restraining "new culture of health and body maintenance" – as proof of possessing good cultural capital – with the older "culture of extravagance" typical of a more traditional leisure class, characterized by excess and indulgence, largely based on a predilection for heavy drinking, as a proof of pecuniary power.

This coexistence of contradictory eating styles has become a hallmark of postmodern lifestyles, emblematically and extremely embodied in the 1980s by "yuppies," but now perfectly integrated into the apps and affordances installed on our smartphones. The double attitude of indulging one day and dieting the next outlines a sort of calculated decontrol (Featherstone, 1991, p. 20). By offering people a wide range of choices in a scheme of self-discipline means training individuals to the ideological program of consumer sovereignty largely based on a strategic ability to move in and out of self-control, so as to experience a wider range of sensations and enhance the propensity to consume. Food intake paradigmatically responds to this scheme of symbolic differentiation, a trait of the postmodern individual – and consequently consumer – based on the conceptualization of the self as a conscious project, that is brought to regard common practices (restraint and control in eating behaviors) as regimes of self-monitoring or self-surveillance (Wernick, 1991).

Moreover, the health/indulgence antinomy is particularly marked by gender differences, with women tending to be more prone to healthy eating, while men are more likely to privilege indulgent behaviors due to a more showy and materialistic approach to food. There is ample literature demonstrating this gender difference in food-related values. One notable study is Schwartz's (2005), which shows that men attribute more importance to values such as power, stimulation, hedonism, achievement, and self-direction, while women place greater emphasis on benevolence and universalism values, and to a lesser extent, on security values. Both sexes show similar attitudes toward tradition and conformity values. Advertisers are well aware of this difference, continuing to use women's testimonials to promote yogurt or any other type of healthy food, while using men to promote indulgent or decadent foods.

2.1.3 *Extravagance versus economy reviewed*

Another dilemma typically faced by the middle-class consumer involves the conflict between economy and extravagance (Warde, 1997, pp. 97–125), with the latter representing an ostentatious form of indulgence. The social dimension primarily involved in this dilemma is money.

2.1.3.1 Extravagance: No break for pangolins, even amid the pandemic

Extravagance is the materialistic and to an extent "conspicuous" side of indulgency, that, in these terms, works as an antinomy of "economy" meant as nonexpensive. Typically, extravagance is expressed through privileging luxury goods. As Warde (1997, p. 102) highlights, in many societies, being able to eat copiously and well on a regular basis has been a sign of privilege.

As both Veblen's (1899) and Bourdieu's (1984) sociological accounts demonstrate, food can readily become a factor of social distinction within an emulative dynamic based on "invidious comparison" with individuals positioned higher in the hierarchy. The inclination toward extravagance reflects a taste pattern typically cultivated within this mechanism of social distinction. By responding to this need of displaying pecuniary assets through wasting money on expensive goods, luxury is a distinctive factor conveying exclusivity and a sense of social superiority.

Some foodstuffs are primarily known for their expense: caviar, lobster, and truffles, for instance, are classical examples of the so-called "Veblen goods," also known as "positional goods" (Hirsch, 1977) wherein the more they cost, the more they are sought after and consumed. Their high price conveys rarity and exquisiteness ("recherché"), symbolizing the privilege of upper classes to access surplus and reflecting the pretentious aspirations of the middle-class upper echelons. These status-oriented, rarity-based, extravagant consumer choices, though mitigated by increasing awareness of the harmful effects on the environment or species involved, are still prevalent in many parts of the world. While furs are no longer a status symbol in most Western societies, purchasing parts of rare wild species remains a status-affirming choice in South-Eastern countries. This behavior persists despite the potential global consequences, as demonstrated by the outbreak of a pandemic originating from a wet market in Wuhan, where pangolins and bats are sold for human consumption.

Research conducted during the pre-COVID pandemic era by USAID (The United States Agency for International Development) focused on illegal trafficking in wild species and the persistent consumer demand for elephant, rhino, and pangolin parts and products in South-Eastern countries, such as China and Vietnam (USAID, 2018; USAID & Traffic, 2020).[5] This research demonstrates that status is the main reason for the demand for items such as pangolin meat, rhino horn, and tiger bone wine (Menon et al., 2019). Parts or meat of these animals play a significant social role, indicating wealth or social status while providing a sense of belonging. They also offer other benefits such as high investment value and are conducive to business relationships. In fact, research conducted between 2014 and 2020 shows that buyers are most likely to be male, between thirty-five and fifty-five years of age, with middle to high incomes, purchasing these products for conspicuous consumption to display wealth (USAID, 2018; USAID and Traffic, 2020).

Sociology, particularly Bourdieu's account of the strategic display of taste in mass society, illuminates the fact that discerning patterns in food purchases are no longer solely determined by cost or rarity, but by the deployment of symbols that are not considered exclusive merely due to their price, but rather by their association with the tastes of influential social groups. Hence, the appeal to extravagance can take different forms, losing something in terms of bizarre exceptionalism while gaining something in terms of refinement and taste discernment, especially when targeted at middle-class consumers. They, in fact, are heavily engaged in emulative consumer competition, where food expenditure competes for value based on the ostentation of awareness around the details of the characteristics of the same consumer object, resulting in a great fragmentation of taste. Indeed, as Warde notes:

---

[5] The reports of this research are available at the following links: USAID 2018 is at: https://www.usaidrdw.org/resources/reports/inbox/ussv-quant-report-saving-elephants-pangolins-and-rhinos-20181105.pdf/view; USAID & Traffic 2020 is at: https://www.usaidrdw.org/resources/reports/inbox/cwt-digest-iii/view. Both have been accessed on 09/06/2024.

> Some households eat more expensive versions of the same items - better cuts of meat, or wine; and some households have more cosmopolitan tastes than others, which they share with their perceived peers and in which they may invest considerable identity value. (Warde, 1997, p. 124)

Similar to indulgence, extravagance is also largely associated with eating out, while it is less commonly referenced in recipe columns (or, nowadays, websites) aimed at domestic food preparation. As a matter of fact, taste, namely, the capacity to engage in aesthetic judgment about the object of consumption, is a feature of well-educated social groups who devote a large part of their life or leisure to restaurants as social occasions. As we know well, possessing knowledge and the ability to engage in small talk about food and restaurants reflects a cultural capital acquired through extensive worldly experience and reliable social connections (acquaintances, everyday interactions, and travel) – a practice particularly beneficial for individuals who entertain clients, travel frequently, or regularly dine out with colleagues.

A typical example of a food item associated with claims of distinction is wine. In many countries, wine used to be a product associated with expense, mystery, and snobbery. This perception persists today, as it has become a product of mass consumption among those where its characteristics dictate: the older the wine, the higher its value; the higher the price, the greater the demand. Despite wine becoming a popular drink nowadays, it still retains some of its former associations with connoisseurship and style, being predominantly consumed by the professional segment of the middle class. Knowledge of wine remains a marker of social distinction.

2.1.3.2 Economy: The resurgence of "thrifty" in the era of nonwaste

Opposite to extravagance, the category of "economy" hints at inexpensive goods, where "inexpensive" has the double meaning of "cheap," which does not necessarily exclude indulgence or waste, and "thrifty," generally meaning nonwasteful, parsimonious.

Cheap food evokes concepts such as affordability, easy availability, and accessibility, in contrast to the rarity that characterizes expensive and luxury food. However, in the globalized market, "cheap" has gained a pejorative meaning, associated with highly standardized, large-scale production, and imported food. "Cheap" is also a characteristic of food perceived as poor quality, unhealthy, or unsafe to eat, epitomized by the word "fast."

But we cannot forget that cheap meant as simple, inexpensive foods has always been deemed as a virtue laden with a positive value, even in consumeristic society. For instance, good housewifery has always been associated with paying careful attention to the cost of ingredients, adopting ways for ensuring that all nutritious foodstuffs were used up, and knowing how to make use of gluts of a particular food.

Nowadays, this sense of economy is once again valued by a broad segment of the population, no longer limited to housewives of the lower and middle classes. Instead, it has become a global concern, aligning with the concepts of affordability and inclusivity as outlined in the inequality reduction expectations of the global sustainable goals set by the 2030 UN agenda (United Nations, 2017). Affordability stands out among the priorities of the EU Farm to Fork strategy, particularly in relation to ensuring a sufficient supply of affordable food for citizens as part of robust and resilient food systems (EU, 2020, p. 4). One of the challenges of the EU's Green Deal will be ensuring food security, which means making sure that everyone has access to sufficient, nutritious, sustainable food that upholds high standards of safety and quality, plant health, and animal health and welfare, while meeting dietary needs and food preferences. Preserving the affordability of food for the average consumer while generating fairer economic returns in the supply chain is essential. Ultimately, the goal is to make the most sustainable food also the most affordable, thereby fostering the competitiveness of the EU supply sector, promoting fair trade, creating new business opportunities, and ensuring the integrity of the single market and occupational health and safety (EU, 2020, p. 7). In many other passages of the Farm to Fork strategy document, we find statements that a sustainable food system must guarantee a sufficient and diverse supply of safe, nutritious, affordable, and sustainable food to people at all times, especially during crises (p. 12). The food industry and retail sector should lead by example by increasing the availability and affordability of healthy, sustainable food options at a price that is affordable for everyone (p. 13).

However, this objective of affordability, price, and economic solutions is facing challenges, as the costs of the ecological transition and its affordability impact the weakest segments of society, especially in the initial phase. Because of this, price and economy, seen as opposites of green and sustainable initiatives, are arguments inflamed and exploited by Euroskeptical political parties, often coming to the center of many protests.

Nevertheless, advocating for economy in the economy-extravagance dilemma, especially when associated with thrift and nonwaste, has become a symbol of awareness and cultural capital. It is no longer solely associated with the economic constraints affecting popular stands but is embraced by the elites as a trait of mindfulness and foresight. According to the "trickle-down" paradigm of cultural transmission of taste (Triggs, 2001), during times of ecological transition, elites, by embracing thrifty, nonwasteful, and inconspicuous food choices, may spearhead cultural change and establish the norms of sustainable fashion and consumption.

2.1.4 *Care versus Convenience revisited*

This dilemma alludes to the oppositions between food meant as a commodity, demanding less effort in both the preparation and consumption phases, and food as a labor of love, demanding a lot of attention and devotion, particularly in the phase of preparation (Warde, 1997, pp. 126–154). It is clear that the dimension involved in this dilemma is time: the time needed to invest in the food item as a meal prepared with love, or as a meal suitable for busy lifestyles. Saving time is a dimension of food practices introduced by commodification, as exemplified by food processing and commercial brewing, which changed the modes of household food supply and reduced labor. The effects of such commodification of food on taste patterns is something that remains frequently unrecognized, since consumption studies tend to neglect what happens to goods after they leave the shop, and focus on preference only at the point of sale.

Convenience and the decline of food preparation at home marked late-modern societies, where home kitchens had been reduced to functional spaces (Cieraad, 1999), and supermarkets represented the "quick and easy" solution, offering the widest possible variety of items (often precooked, preweighed, etc.) in a single shop. The outbreak of the COVID-19 pandemic and the extended confinement at home led to a rediscovery of the home kitchen as a space for spending time on cooking, reviving its significance as a hub for family socialization and cooking as a form of entertainment rather than just a chore (Onorati et al., 2023).

This exceptional event cast light on the polarization between convenience as the cold and impersonal world of capitalist rationalization and commodification of time – especially free time, including eating time turned into a "break" – on one side, and care as the homely meal prepared with familiar (i.e., motherly) love, on the other side. This dilemma epitomizes more than one contradiction in our society through which gender divides in the roles of family care have been played: The tension between viewing household cooking as an instrumental and technical activity, as the prerogative of men, as opposed to cooking as a labor of love – a creative and expressive act of lavishing care – as the prerogative of women (DeVault, 1991).

2.1.4.1 Care as a perduring gap among genders

Home cooking is a meaningful way to cherish a family. Care in food practices refers to the love manifested by providing the family with the meals they enjoy (insofar as the budget allows). Even if the process of commodification reduces the amount of labor time devoted to feeding, it still represents a fundamental form of care. In many societies, most of this responsibility still falls to women, even in the most emancipated areas. According to the European Index of Gender Equality, in 2022, women still performed 63% of the daily time devoted to cooking or doing housework (Figure 2). This means that two out of three people caring for feeding the family at home within an EU country are women[6].

Food is an expression of love, and a sacrifice too, it is a labor of love. One effect is that through the family meal, the person who cooks, typically women, produce the family itself. The most insightful study of the caring aspect of domestic food provision is DeVault's Feeding the Family (1991). In DeVault's words:

> [...] the feeding work traditionally undertaken by women is both produced by and produces "family" as we have known it- the work itself "feeds" not only household members but also "the family" as ideological construct (DeVault, 1991, p. 236).

---

[6] Data about EIGE 2023 dimensions are available at the following link: https://eige.europa.eu/gender-equality-index/2023/domain/time (accessed on 09/06/2024).

Figure 2   People doing cooking and/or housework, every day by gender
(% 18–74 population)

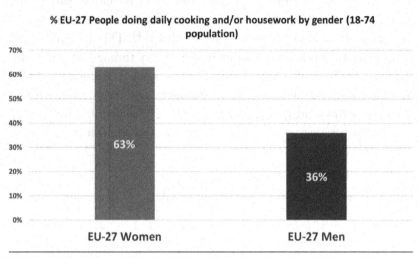

Source: EIGE's survey on unpaid care, 2022. Author's adapted graph on EIGE's calculations.

Feeding a family encompasses more than just the physical upkeep of household members; it also involves the day-to-day cultivation of connection and sociability. Care for and care about are intricately intertwined in enduring personal relationships, such as those within families. Food provisioning and the organization of food-related events play pivotal roles in both the construction and perpetuation of familial bonds. The emotional significance attached to food provision within the family may suggest a resistance to commodification in itself. Unfortunately, this socially significant labor remains unrecognized and unpaid, thereby undermining its importance.

2.1.4.2 Convenience: The queen of recipe websites

Although food preparation involves emotional dimensions, the commodification and rationalization of food production have caused cooking to become a more technical matter. It is now seen as the result of effective performance, demonstrating culinary expertise or knowledge about food, with less emotional expression of familial care and concern. Since the end of the sixties, there has been a declining value placed upon care with explicit reference to family food and homemade meals in public and commercial discourse about food. In fact, food, as a labor of love, demands time, and nowadays people's time has become increasingly scarce. The leisure class finds themselves "harried," and the complex interrelationship of money, time, and goods that besets consumer society has infiltrated the kitchen. As highlighted by Bourdieu (1984, p. 186), convenience has been the option of the emancipated middle class endowed with high cultural capital, particularly of women engaged in reorganizing the time balance between life and work.

The reduction in time devoted to food, driven by convenience, is partly due to the shifting roles in family care and partly to the commodification of food production and consumption. This has bestowed upon "convenient" an ambiguous meaning. Food items might be, or be perceived as, convenient in many ways: The ease with which a product may be prepared, served, and eaten; simplicity in the cooking process; speedy cooking, cooking without special utensils, serving without cooking; using the product in combination with many different things or to different sorts of people on different kinds of meal occasions. Convenience may also involve ease of acquisition through being available at a large number of retail outlets, being easily stored and available for use at any time (Gofton and Ness, 1991, pp. 20–21).

Although time, especially time-saving, is an important dimension of lifestyles in consumeristic society, the term "convenient" is rarely openly used in commercial language to recommend a dish, as it may be perceived as offensive, implying insufficient care toward the family. In fact, almost all recipe websites from around the world have a section named "quick and easy," alluding to convenient preparations without openly labeling them as such.

This food-related dilemma is of the utmost importance within social sciences because it alludes to a relevant dimension of societal life: Time. Social scientists often use time-budget techniques to explore such matters. Social surveys frequently ask household members to provide information about the time spent on each of their daily activities, often by keeping detailed diaries recording them.

The sociologically relevant dimensions entailed by the dilemma food care or food convenience are time-saving and easy. Convenient recipes prioritize speed, often promoting the use of tinned foods, frozen items, or ready-to-eat meals that can be quickly heated in the microwave. The term "quick," often associated with "easy," has become a common descriptor for such recipes, where the short time required for preparation and the ease of cooking are emphasized as technical aspects both in the dish itself and in the accompanying videos, as evident on various recipe websites. Social media further accentuates the importance of speed, as it's a fundamental requirement for generating interest in showcased recipes and ensuring their popularity. This emphasis on speed is also necessary to accommodate the short duration of reels and their visual presentation. Storage is another indicator of convenience, as certain dishes can be stored for future use. This characteristic not only helps save time during the provisioning phase but also proves to be more compatible with weekly visits to the supermarket. Snacking, grazing, brunch, and happy hours: These eating occasions exemplify the sociological implications of contemporary eating patterns. These habits, which include the increasing prevalence of snacking or grazing, the convenience of brunch as a fusion of breakfast and lunch, and the popularity of happy hours often replacing dinner, reflect the diverse range of convenient eating events occurring outside households, typically in restaurants, pubs, cafes, and take-away food outlets. These activities absorb a significant proportion of the time expenditure on food.

The time on cooking and gender divides

As said before, emphasis on care or convenience involves patterns of domestic divisions of labor within couple households, because the amount of time devoted to household labor plays a large part in any understanding of the organization of food provisioning and eventually of the unequal distribution of tasks among family members. Cooking can be a chore, a drudgery activity, if perceived as an obligation or part of an unequal distribution of care roles, or a pleasure as an intrinsically enjoyable and pleasing activity, that involves not only knowledge and practical skills but also creativity, and even a form of gift-giving.

Time reduction in food preparation has become, then, part of such important manifestations of role taking in family life with a strong sociological meaning, because it can cast light on tensions surrounding the definition of ideals of womanhood, between wife–mother and the autonomous person.

In order to investigate this touchy dimension, surveys generally inquire as to who "usually does particular tasks" or who did the task last (Warde et al., 1989). The evidence that the socially significant labor of family care, specifically cooking, continues to fall disproportionately on women and remains unrecognized and unpaid underscores another gender divide in the public sphere of gastronomy. Here, women's culinary contributions are often depicted as amateur, while men's work is portrayed as highly professional. One might observe that cooking shows hosted by women often replicate the ambiance of a home kitchen, fostering a sense of familiarity and comfort, typical of amateur contexts. By contrast, shows hosted by men tend to feature more neutral settings, resembling technical spaces filled with appliances geared toward competitive cooking. These environments are sometimes depicted as high-pressure atmospheres, reminiscent of hells – think Gordon Ramsay's "Hell's Kitchen."

We anticipated that the rise of the internet and social media would bridge the gap, and to some extent, it did. However, the representation and positioning of men and women in the public sphere of recipe websites continue to exhibit a stark divide between female-amateur and male-professional expertise. A notable instance can be found on the renowned Italian recipe platform "Giallozafferano," where the section featuring recipes by top professional chefs is dominated by men,[7] while the section dedicated to food bloggers is predominantly occupied by women, reflecting the perception of blogging as a more personal, amateur pursuit akin to diary writing.[8]

Time-saving and time-consuming meals: What about health?
If our society assigns different moral significance to eating activities based on whether they are time-consuming or time-saving, it does not necessarily indicate which of these activities are healthier or more recommendable. Carefully prepared home-cooked meals do not always equate to healthier options. Time-consuming meal preparations often involve elaborate processes and numerous ingredients, which can result in high-calorie dishes. However, the amount of time spent on preparation is not necessarily indicative of the nutritional value of a meal. Conversely, time-saving options may not always prioritize nutrition. In fact, a diet exclusively reliant

---

[7] Please visit the following link: https://www.giallozafferano.it/le-ricette-degli-chef/ (accessed on 09/06/2024).
[8] Visit the following link: https://www.giallozafferano.it/ricette-top-blogger/ (accessed on 09/06/2024).

on packaged and preprepared frozen foods from supermarkets may be more convenient but could be less nutritious and higher in fat, sodium, sugar compared to meticulously prepared home-cooked meals. Additionally, regardless of quality, all types of meals, from the finest to the least nutritious, can be easily purchased ready-made in restaurants, sandwich shops, and take-away outlets, albeit at a higher price.

The concept of convenience in the food sector is undergoing considerable change due to technological progress. A new era of convenience is expected to emerge as technology rationalizes meal planning, shopping, and cooking.

Brands have tailored their products to help consumers maximize their kitchen efficiency, demonstrated by cooking guides for various appliances and product lines designed to cook multiple items simultaneously at the same temperature. Looking forward, consumers' positive experiences with these efficient products and appliances will make them more receptive to new time-saving technologies. This shift will transform conveniences like automated shopping lists and meal planning apps from optional extras to essential daily tools.

Technologies such as AI and AR in food preparation and consumption will provide a range of solutions to meet diverse consumer needs. These technologies will assist in finding the perfect balance between times when consumers want to craft innovative and engaging dishes, drinks, and snacks, and moments when meal planning, shopping, cooking, or even eating can be handled automatically (Mintel, 2024b, p. 15).

2.2   The evolution of food taste dilemmas in times of crisis and ecological transition

Since 1997, food taste patterns identified as antinomies have evolved in tandem with shifting consumer demands and increased awareness.

In the time of the omnivore's dilemma and ecological catastrophe, the contradictory dilemmas gripping consumers regarding food should evolve into a new mindfulness no longer based on a binary vision of the world. In post-anthropocentric times, the productive challenge for a social theory should tackle issues no longer conceived in binary terms, but rather address them as emerging from intercultural dialogues and multi-layered perspectives.

Particularly, these dilemmas should be reconsidered in light of the current era, where human centrality is shifting toward what is referred to as the Eco-Anthropocene (Clark, 2015). This concept represents the post-anthropocentric evolution of the term Anthropocene, which emerged around the year 2000, conveying the idea that humanity has gained the ability to influence the biophysical dynamics of the planet, thereby directly impacting them (Crutzen and Stoermer, 2000). Eco-Anthropocene, or ecological-eco-political Anthropocene, means considering an alternative Anthropocene, which is itself a "threshold concept" (Clark, 2015), involving a new perspective on social and more-than-human relations, grounded in humility and respect (Pellizzoni, 2022), and incorporating constant feedback from the ecosystem in addressing human issues.

The overarching question is whether such dualisms still hold relevance in an era where all Western ontological dualisms (such as mind/body, subject/object, natural/artificial, sensuous/ideal, living/nonliving, male/female, and active/passive) are critiqued as theoretically untenable and morally and politically objectionable due to their implicit hierarchical implications, each binary system suggesting the superiority of one aspect over the other. Unfortunately, the increasing polarization of values shaping people's choices, particularly in the realm of food, demonstrates that these antinomies have not vanished from public discourse or from individuals' minds; rather, they have been revised.

Political marketing, especially, exploits people's uncertainties regarding their decision-making motivations in terms of these antinomies, presenting a simplified version of the contradictions inherent in the world and exerting influence over their choices. Understanding the complexity underlying consumer behavior through the lens of antinomies helps recognize and comprehend the contradictions that define contemporary landscapes, particularly within the realm of foodscapes.

How are taste antinomies evolving in the age of the Eco-Anthropocene? Care has found its way back into the handling of food in many respects. One important aspect is self-care, where food is used as a preventative measure to reduce health risks. The Food and Agriculture Organization of the United Nations (FAO) definition of sustainable nutrition highlights the evolution and complexity of people's priorities in relation to their diet:

Sustainable diets are those diets with low environmental impacts which contribute to food and nutrition security and to healthy life for present and future generations. Sustainable diets are protective and respectful of biodiversity and ecosystems, culturally acceptable, accessible, economically fair and affordable; nutritionally adequate, safe and healthy; while optimizing natural and human resources. (FAO, 2012)

This definition takes particular account of the four dimensions of sustainable nutrition: (1) health, (2) economy, (3) social and cultural aspects, and (4) environment (Drewnowski, 2018). Sustainable diets not only have a low impact on the environment but are also healthy, affordable, and acceptable to society. While nutritional metrics and environmental impact indices exist to determine the level of sustainability and healthiness of a diet, the affordability, acceptability, and desire for a sustainable, healthy diet are solely determined by sociocultural factors (Monterrosa et al., 2020) and likely take the form of contradictions within society and dilemmas in the minds of consumers. They need a sociological approach that understands them as evolving antinomies of taste.

Consequently, we can assert that in contemporary times, in addition to the original four, at least four more dilemmas guide consumer priorities: global/local, fake/authentic, ethical/unethical, and eco-friendly/noneco-friendly. A fifth concern, that is, risky/safe, has gained prominence, especially following the health emergency of 2020.

2.2.1 SAFE versus RISKY

This dilemma is likely the reconfiguration of the Health vs. Indulgence antinomy in times of environmental catastrophe and health emergency. Global market insights show that consumer priorities and behaviors have focused on self-care since the outbreak of the COVID-19 pandemic, with safe and healthy food being top of mind for consumers (Euromonitor 2020, 2021a).

We have already highlighted the evolution of health concerns into the adoption of healthy lifestyles, facilitated by the pervasive integration of digital devices and their affordances in our daily activities. In general, artificial intelligence can help determine the best diet for each individual, particularly when integrated into quality labeling schemes. According to Euromonitor (2021b), the pandemic "new normal" saw 64% of consumers worldwide believe that wellness is the highest priority for overall health. Older cohorts, in particular, have shifted to using technology that offers customized "health sentinel" services to track health data in real time and identify potential health threats as quickly as possible. In this increasingly health-focused mentality, eating has become a mindful activity, and food is seen as medicine.

Actually, even before the outbreak of the pandemic, concern for health had already entered the consumer mindset as part of a call for a more responsible lifestyle, shifting health concerns into a demand for safety. The controversial NutriScore front-of-package labeling system developed in France in 2017, which provides information about the nutritional quality of packaged foods by assigning a color-coded letter score (A to E) to the product, is an example of how the market is responding to this renewed concern about safety. The transformation of health concerns into safety guarantees also attests to consumers' emotional overlaying of their demands for informed consumption in troubled times.

In quite uncertain times, the dilemma between safety and risk extends to encompass many other conflicting options in consumer decision-making, epitomizing deeper, more primal fears. The dichotomy of safety vs. risk also represents the contemporary ideological iteration of the novelty/tradition antinomy. We have already referred to the ambiguous perception of novel food by lay consumers, which is rejected because it is perceived as risky – a mixture of unsafe and unfamiliar. When consumers are faced with the conflicting choice of trying something new vs. sticking with familiar choices while grocery shopping, it transforms into a question: Do we embrace change and venture into the risky unknown, or do we play it safe, adhering to our familiar habits? Politics or corporate interests can easily exploit these uncertainties and dilemmas among consumers, amplifying them with discourses that easily polarize positions.

Consider the strongly polarizing discussion about "risky" cultured-cell meat, awkwardly conflated with the generic term "novel food" and fueled by flyers distributed during the summer of 2023 by Coldiretti, the largest association of Italian farmers (Figure 4). This campaign, which presented cultured meat as a risky, unethical, and unnatural result of technological exploitation and mishandling of nature, rallied consensus around easily polarized categories of "good-nature" vs. "bad-science." This sentiment was further supported by the law against cultivated meat production, which was promulgated at the end of 2023.

2.2.2 *FAKE versus AUTHENTIC*

Fake *vs.* Authentic products is an emerging dilemma that opens a door
not only to a renewed call for trustworthy care over unreliable convenience but also to the reassuring identity appeal of careful tradition,
shaping consumer demand for food, particularly in times of crisis, and
to the insatiable desire for pronounced exclusivity despite the crisis. In
this sense, we can consider authentic *vs.* fake as another updated version
of care *vs.* convenience, as well as novelty *vs.* tradition and economy *vs.*
extravagance. Authentic food means that it is internal to a culinary tradition (Heldke, 2005), making it a characteristic of food that can easily
leverage sentiments about identity and care – claims that have become
critical in troubled times. Authenticity recalls care when it qualifies food
as embedded in a national or regional culinary tradition, making it a
whole of flavors and ingredients tied to a familiar heritage of rituals and
practices that are part of identity.

Because of all these elements, authenticity is perceived as a predominantly positive characteristic based on qualities such as geographic distinctiveness, "simplicity," and personal connections – all qualities that
express distinction (in Bourdieu's sense of the word) from the generic,
faceless, mass-produced, inauthentic mainstream (Johnston and Baumann, 2007, 2010). Authenticity is one of the demands of today's consumers because it provides a framework for understanding worthy and
legitimate food preferences, and recognizing authenticity is a way to confer status without seeming like snobbery (Johnston and Baumann 2007,
p. 178). This is probably why "authentic" emerged as the most digitized
word in 2023.[9] It is also the reason why certificates of origin have become
a crucial factor in quality systems, turning from strategies to safeguard
products from imitation into real mythologies of assumed superiority and
imagined communities.

The term "authentic" was introduced in the food market in the 1990s
as part of a strategy to protect some traditional products from manipulation and imitation in the global market. With Council Regulation
(EEC) No. 2081/92 of July 14, 1992, the European Commission in-

---

[9] See: https://www.merriam-webster.com/wordplay/word-of-the-year (accessed
on 30/05/2024).

troduced the European logos PDO (Protected Designation of Origin), PGI (Protected Geographical Indication), and TSG (Traditional Specialty Guaranteed), establishing them as schemes to promote and safeguard certain food products by tying their quality to the regional areas where they are produced or primarily processed (European Communities, 1992). In the same period (1991), the EU also started a process of recognition and certification of Organic Farming as a specific Quality Assurance Scheme (QAS), characterized by voluntary participation and a clearly defined assurance of both product and process quality, although a clear regulation about the use of EU-logo labeling for organic produce started only in 2007.[10]

The EU quality schemes aimed at safeguarding rural diversity and promote regional agricultural products through the designation of product's origin and geographical indications labeled on the packaging. These logos certify the unique link not only between a product and a tradition or a typicality but also between a product and a place or a geographical area through a recognized know-how that is considered exclusive to the designated area and therefore should be protected from imitation. Although it is debatable whether this exclusive association with geographical areas is a guarantee of protection for the smaller farmers engaged in typical products (Fino and Cecconi, 2021, p. 32; Welz, 2013), it is clear that these logos have become an important marketing strategy to "brand" places and transform them from typical production sites to tourist destinations (Marcoz et al., 2016; Gordin and Trabskaya, 2013; Lai et al., 2019).

Authenticity, especially in conjunction with a labeling strategy, also recalls integrity, which is one of the components of trust and credibility, two crucial factors in the relationship with the consumer that are at risk in times of crisis. For these many reasons, authenticity has become a prominent part of "credence qualities" (Grunert and Aachmann 2016) that shape consumer expectations of quality, and guide consumption choices. This simple reference to trustworthiness is why authenticity is

---

[10] On this topic, please see Council Regulation (EC) No 834/2007 of June 28, 2007 on organic production and labelling of organic products and repealing Regulation (EEC) No 2092/91, available at: https://eur-lex.europa.eu/eli/reg/2007/834/oj (accessed on 30/05/2024).

an attribute that predominates, especially in social media, in amateur food criticism, a communicative space where credibility of food appreciation is based less on expert judgment than on a holistically perceived food experience (Rousseau, 2012; Kobez, 2018, 2020; Weatherell et al., 2003, p. 243). Thus, the characteristic of authenticity, often "sealed" by an origin logo placed on the package, attests to the superior quality of a product as it is closely tied to the land and tradition. Initially designed to preserve a direct relationship with the land and its producers, authenticity has evolved into a marker for exclusive and expensive products, marginalizing small-scale farmers and low-income consumers. Discriminating between authentic and fake products also distinguishes skilled consumers or food critics from the mass. In this context, the higher price that distinguishes PDOs from PGIs, TSGs, or DOGCs from DOCs contributes to making authenticity a contemporary – and to a certain extent, less ostentatious but still eyebrow-raising – alternative to extravagance, while fake becomes a modern interpretation of economy, thus functioning in consumer culture as an updated marker of distinction (Johnston and Baumann, 2007, 2010; Onorati and Giardullo, 2020).

Authenticity is also a claim featuring primarily consumers from countries with a strong culinary tradition, such as France, Italy, and Spain, which also count the higher number of origin-labeled products in the EU region.[11] For these consumers, especially Italians, authentic food means not only drawing on a vast cultural repertoire but also honoring the value of originality and beauty that is part of a tradition and even of a national sentiment. Of course, everything outside the perimeter of labeled authentic food, which is also a geographic boundary, is perceived antinomically as faceless, foreign, untrustworthy, in a word: "fake." This is why, from 2020 onwards, the nationalistic sentiment of Italian consumers has overridden the demand for quality, and the preference for products simply labeled as Italian has surpassed that for EU-origin labels of these products (Figure 3). Identity is back.

---

[11] Intro: https://www.qualivita.it/osservatorio/osservatorio- ue/ (accessed on 30/05/2024).

Figure 3 Evolving food consumer trends in Italy based on the type of food
certification

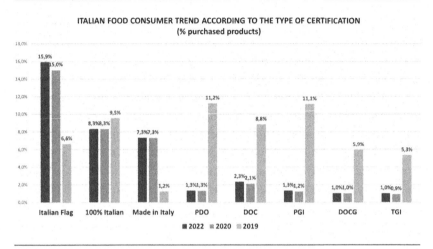

Source: Author's adaptation of *Dati Osservatorio Immagino OI 2022 – GS1 Italy*. Calculated
on 90,000 products.[12]

2.2.3. *GLOBAL versus LOCAL*

This conflict in consumer choices is closely intertwined with the opposition between authentic and inauthentic, yet it more effectively encapsulates the growing trend of identity assertion among consumers depicted in Figure 3. The dilemma of global *vs.* local is directly linked to identity, expressing demands and sentiments for what is perceived as closer, familiar, and "ours" – characteristics that are only partially conveyed through authenticity. This dilemma represents the current evolution of the conflict between tradition and novelty.

For these reasons, "local" is often associated with localism and a protective sense of community, making "locavorism" susceptible to the ideological glorification of sovereigntist and antiglobalization sentiments during global crises (Onorati and d'Ovidio, 2022; Reich et al., 2018). It also acquires the connotation of originality attributed to authenticity, be-

---

[12] See also: https://gs1it.org/servizi/osservatorio-immagino/ (accessed on 01/09/2022).

ing rooted in the tradition of a place where origin becomes synonymous with quality.

Locavorism reveals a dual, even contradictory mindset among consumers: on one side, it addresses communal or safety concerns driven by embedded and conservative values against an outside perceived as dangerous and extraneous; on the other side, the preference for local foods also reflects a biospheric sensibility that was already gaining momentum before the pandemic outbreak and has become predominant in consumer behavior in recent years, partly due to policy strategies prioritizing short supply chains. The preference for local food is not merely about evoking a gloomy, nostalgic past or a static identity, but rather a response to ecological concerns such as zero-kilometer sourcing, seasonality, and biodiversity, particularly when associated with its most obvious benefit, freshness (Schulp, 2015, p. 130).

2.2.4 *ETHICAL versus UNETHICAL*

Ethical *vs.* Unethical and its variant Fair *vs.* Unfair represent the contemporary version of the care/convenience dilemma. As discussed previously, while convenience is not inherently negative in food choices, it is rarely cited as a positive qualification of products, often replaced by less self-directed adjectives like "quick" and "easy." Indeed, for long time, convenience has been the option of the emancipated middle class endowed with high cultural capital, particularly of women engaged in reorganizing the time balance between life and work (Bourdieu, 1984, p. 186). Time is a crucial dimension in this dilemma, where diligence is a synonym for time-consuming, slow, while convenience means time-saving, fast. We are well aware that the terms "fast" and "slow," especially in the food system, allude to alternative paradigms. The fast paradigm, as described by Ritzer in his masterpiece McDonaldization (1998), is the negative epitome of a distracted, consumerist society in which food is completely subject to the logic of commodification and standardization, both on the side of production and consumption. In this sense, fast has come to allude to a scarce attention to people or nature in the name of an unresponsible, even unhealthy, model of production and consumption. Slow, on the contrary, also thanks to the food activism revolving around the Slow Food movement, is a term that gained positive meanings in the last decades, referring to a responsible use of resources, holistic understanding of the human/nature relationship and safeguard of bio-cultural diversity of food as a benchmark of quality (Petrini, 2005). All of this requires adequate time and space, along with a strong connection with the territory and community in the production model. This evolution has led to a preference for local supply chains over long ones, which proved to be vulnerable during critical times such as pandemics. Whether taking all these dimensions into account leads to a more equitable and inclusive model on the production side does not necessarily mean a more inclusive model on the consumption side.

As argued by Paddock (2016), the appreciation of local foods' embeddedness (Murdoch et al., 2000), the relationships between producers and consumers (Kneafsey et al., 2008), and everything labelled as "slow" run the risk of turning food into a mere aestheticization of food (Miele and Murdoch, 2002), confined within the contemporary expression of alternative food, as long as it remains inaccessible and unaffordable. Ethical food remains a niche product, available in limited fair-trade circles, out of reach or difficult to access for lower or disadvantaged segments of society. This becomes especially evident when the concept of consuming "alternative" foods is presented as the sole path to "good" and "correct" food, and is employed as a means of drawing boundaries between social groups. In this context, the privilege of being able to afford or possess knowledge about these alternative foods may turn consumption choices into a way to assert a sense of ethical superiority, cloaking their socioeconomic advantage under the guise of ethical behavior. This dilemma thus opens up a great deal of thinking about the inclusivity and exclusivity of consumption, echoing Bauman's warning that consumption can create new forms of stratification and perpetuate social exclusion by dividing people into the "haves" and "have-nots" (Bauman, 1998).

2.2.5 *ECO-FRIENDLY versus ECO-NON-FRIENDLY*

Ecological transition is both a crucial objective for the future of our societies and planet, as well as a source of significant political debate surrounding European environmental policies. Much of the European green vision is stated in the so-called "Farm to fork" strategy, the programmatic document about building sustainable EU food systems, in line with the EU's Green Deal. Launched in May 2020, its measures are moving at different speeds, sparking extensive discussions about its aims and priorities to achieve the goals scheduled by 2030. The EU institutions play a key role in shaping various aspects of this strategy and supporting its measures at different speeds, ensuring alignment with diverse stakeholders, including farmers and consumers. This is clearly stated in the document:

> The Commission will put forward an Action Plan on organic farming. This will help Member States stimulate both supply and demand for organic products. It will ensure consumer trust and boost demand through promotion campaigns and green public procurement. This approach will help to reach the objective of at least 25% of the EU's agricultural land under organic farming by 2030 and a significant increase in organic aquaculture. (Farm to fork, 2020, pp. 10–11)

In the last months, the "Farm to Fork" strategy has faced significant criticism from farmer-led protests fueled by Eurosceptics and populist parties. This criticism sheds light on the challenges of implementing a sustainable food system that must meet the needs of diverse stakeholders while addressing complex, urgent issues such as climate change, loss of biodiversity, and public health concerns.

While it is far beyond the intentions of this study to address the adequacy of the Farm to Fork policy, it is entirely within its scope to illuminate the enduring presence of cultural antinomies behind the polarization and ideological divisions surrounding the complex implementation of ecological transition. These antinomies serve as hidden catalysts, prompting individuals to lose sight of the complexity and take stances either *for* or *against* green policies. The ideological appropriation and amplification of these antinomies, often for political purposes, has resulted in the paradoxical situation where farmers and environmentalists, who should naturally be allies, have become antagonists.

This conflicting attitude outlines an Eco-Friendly *vs.* Eco-Non-Friendly antinomy, which represents an updated evolution of the conflict between care (for the planet and life) and convenience (prioritizing more readily available fuels or conventional fertilizers, which might promise bigger yields in shorter time). This dichotomy, primarily involving risks related to time, intersects with money, resulting in the dilemma between expensive *vs.* economy. The shift toward eco-friendly production systems requires long-term economic investments by producers. In the short term, they face economic stress due to decisions aimed at accelerating the transition, such as reintroducing agricultural taxes, cutting subsidies on conventional agrofuels, increasing insurance policies as a result of climate change, and so on. These maneuvers may not yield immediate benefits, but they are essential for long-term sustainability. They catalyze the dimensions of time and money within the dilemma of eco-friendly *vs.* eco-non-friendly, which also encompasses conflicting ethical decisions. Such polarization easily lends itself to populist, supremacist narratives portraying Europe as the antagonist, the enemy of the underprivileged.

Dividing the world into binary constructs and resurrecting these dilemmas, departing from the inseparable seamless fabric of "nature-culture" (Latour, 1993, p. 7), which constitutes the entirety of collectives (p. 107), perpetuates the polarization of knowledge. This approach imposes micro-assaults by compressing and limiting any capacity to fully and holistically grasp the complexity of things while divorcing them from the broader complexity in which they are embedded. However, this simplification represents the most straightforward path to gaining consensus and is the strategy pursued by power to maintain control over the multitudes. This is what the media campaign by Coldiretti, the largest association of Italian farmers, did when they launched a petition against the introduction of favorable legislation for cultivated meat. Through a masterful marketing operation, they employed a communication strategy that framed the potential consequences of this type of meat production as a discourse based on antinomies. They used a flyer (Figure 4) presenting two contrasting worlds with "*vs.*" to clearly delineate the opposing sides in the imagery.[13]

This two-sided representation catalyzed individual uncertainties and ignorance about a relatively new technique into a polarized vision of the world, split between good *vs.* evil, right *vs.* wrong, shaping and rallying consensus around the upcoming Law No. 172/2023, which bans research, production, and trade of cultivated meat in Italy. The flyer used to prompt people to sign the petition aimed not at providing information or fostering a critical debate on a crucial and complex topic for the future of sustainable food systems, but solely at polarizing people's sentiments by simplifying a complex matter into a misleading dichotomy.

---

[13] Cf. https://www.coldiretti.it/economia/una-firma-contro-il-cibo-sintetico-scatta-la-mobilitazione-coldiretti (accessed on 20/02/2023).

Figure 4   The flyer distributed by Coldiretti, the association of Italian farmers, against cultured-cell-based meat[14]

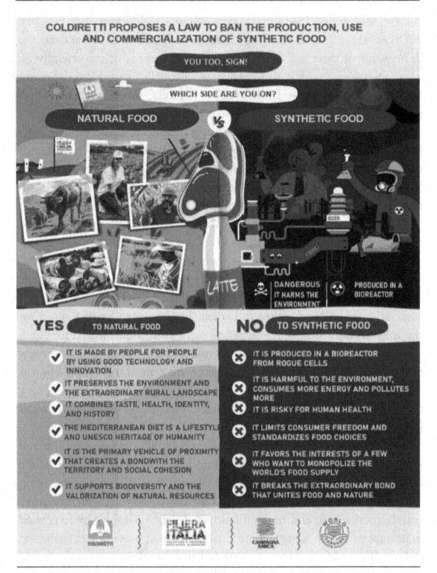

Source: English translated version of the original flyer widespread by Coldiretti against cell-cultured meat.

[14] The text of the flyer has been translated from Italian to English by the author.

How many antinomies are incorporated in this simple flyer? Many, even all of them, starting from the principal one from which all others descend and has been the mark of the anthropocentric paradigm of human progress until now: the conflict between nature and culture.

On one side, presented as "safe," we find a reassuring and bucolic green and yellow rural world where "natural" foods (a cow and salami) are featured prominently – regardless of the fact that animal farming, especially beef herds, produce over 85% of greenhouse gas emissions and that the WHO has declared red meat, particularly processed meats like sausages, as factors that promote the onset of cancer. On the other side, we encounter a dark, "synthetic" world, actually a laboratory scattered with death danger signals where scientists experiment using frightening machinery representing bioreactors in which cells for meat cultivation are grown. This representation is not merely descriptive; it is a petition that asks people to take a stance, either for one side or the other, simplifying such a complex discourse fraught with scientific, economic, and social consequences into an exercise of political marketing.

In the captions that follow, in addition to these antinomies of nature *vs.* culture and safe *vs.* risky, we also find local *vs.* global expressed as a continuum of identity-community-proximity-healthy-Mediterranean diet opposed to distant-global-standardized-disconnected. We also encounter ethical (referring to biodiversity and valorization of the bond with nature) *vs.* unethical (breaking the bond with nature and introducing harmful practices).

Part III
We Eat What We Would Like to Be Like

3   Conspicuousness in Consumption:
Food Taste as a Factor of Social Dynamism

3.1   Veblen and Bourdieu: From leisure to discernment, the internalization of material culture

In sociological terms, considering consumption as a form of social action means moving beyond a mere economic and economistic perspective. According to Aldridge (2003), "consumption is a key concept" in the social sciences because it "unlocks the way" to understanding broader societal dynamics. For sociology, objects are purchased and consumed not solely for their material usefulness or economic efficiency but also for the meanings they convey to buyers and the roles they play within social relationships. Thus, consumer goods attain value as sociological objects when they integrate into the social actions undertaken by individuals based on mutual relationships and societal norms.

Once consumption enters the realms of social action, it can take economically irrational but socially strategic directions. Anticipating two authors very different from each other, such as Baudrillard and Bourdieu, the American sociologist Thorstein Veblen was indeed the first to realize the need to move, in the theory of consumption, from the logic of needs and satisfaction to that of social performance and the production of signs. Veblen provided a sociological explanation of this dynamic by introducing the notion of "conspicuous consumption." This notion would be so successful, to become itself the label of Veblen's theory. Veblen introduced the notion in his 1899 book "The Theory of the Leisure Class," where he argued that consumption choices of affluent classes are often driven more by social status and the desire to display wealth rather than purely practical or utilitarian motives. Particularly, the concept of "conspicuous consumption" provides a critical lens through which to understand the social dynamics of wealth and consumption in industrial societies, particularly during the late nineteenth and early twentieth centuries. This concept emerged against the backdrop of the Second Industrial Revolution in the United States, which saw rapid economic growth, the rise of large corporations, and the formation of a newly affluent middle class. The concentration of wealth in the hands of a few industrial magnates and the rapid emergence of a new wealthy elite characterized the economic conditions of late nineteenth-century American society and became markers of the American dream. The expansion of monopolistic enterprises and business mergers created immense fortunes almost overnight, leading to the phenomenon of "nouveau riche" individuals who sought to assert their newfound status through ostentatious displays of consumption.

During this era of economic expansion and corporate consolidation, conspicuous consumption became a means for individuals striving to ascend the social ladder rapidly by accumulating wealth through business ventures, monopolistic practices, or entrepreneurial success, to assert their newfound affluence. Unlike the established aristocracy, whose wealth was typically inherited, these *nouveaux riches* sought to emulate the lifestyle and status symbols historically associated with old money through lavish spending on leisure activities. Veblen observed that these upper classes, driven by a desire for social emulation and to distinguish themselves within a competitive social hierarchy, engaged in extravagant spending on goods and services that were often unnecessary or wasteful from a practical standpoint but served to visibly demonstrate their wealth and power to others.

Veblen's critique of conspicuous consumption was also a critique of the broader capitalist economy, highlighting how patterns of consumption were shaped not just by individual preferences but also by broader social forces and the pursuit of social distinction. His analysis remains relevant today in discussions about consumer culture, inequality, and the societal implications of materialism and status-seeking behaviors.

Such a historical phenomenon, powerfully represented by F. Scott Fitzgerald in his novel *The Great Gatsby*, published in 1925, was known as the "American dream." This term encapsulates the rise of the American way of life, which began during the "Gilded Age" (1870–1910) and gained momentum in the so-called "Jazz Age" (from World War I to the Great Depression). The "American dream" conjures up the increasing importance of money as a means to rank people in a rapidly changing capitalistic society, as the American society of the early twentieth century was, and found its cultural legitimation in "a blend of the Newtonian belief in a beneficent, finely tuned universe and the American versions of Calvinism and Puritanism, which condoned and encouraged the accumulation of wealth as a way of doing God's work" (Canterbery, 1999, p. 297).

In such a climate of rapid economic expansion, consumption gained sociological relevance since it became part of a dynamic of social mobility based on pecuniary emulation. Veblen's theory of the "leisure class" represents the first sociological account of the rise of conspicuous consumption but also a strong criticism of such a mechanism of pecuniary emulation at the basis of the cutthroat competition fomented by an unbridled capitalism, which led to the accumulation of wealth and capital in a few hands and to their excesses.

Modernization and the economic boom nurtured the illusion that people could aspire to a rapid change in status. By proudly displaying the signs of their success and embracing wasteful and extravagant lifestyles, they sought admission into the restricted echelons of aristocracy. These ideals were epitomized in the tragic story of the fictional character Jay Gatsby, initially created by Fitzgerald's novel and then immortalized through DiCaprio's iconic interpretation in Luhrmann's cinematic adaptation (2013).[1]

Gatsby is a very affluent, self-made man with a mysterious past who disguises his humble origins and pursues money and success, embodying the American Dream during the roaring Twenties. Gatsby is a charismatic figure whose aspirations extend beyond enormous wealth to gaining status and being admitted into the echelons of the leisure class. Longing for Daisy, a wealthy young woman of the leisure class, since he was a poor boy, he ultimately fails to win her hand. Despite accumulating immense wealth by the time of the story, he remains a man without a past, without a "high-ranking genealogy," and the gap between him and his beloved cannot be bridged.

---

[1] "The Great Gatsby," 2013 Australia – USA film directed by Baz Luhrmann, produced by Village Roadshow Pictures, A&E Television, Bazmark Productions Red Wagon Entertainment; Distributed by Warner Bros and roadshow Films (Running time: 142').

Daisy was young and her artificial world was redolent of orchids and pleas-
ant, cheerful snobbery and orchestras which set the rhythm of the year,
summing up the sadness and suggestiveness of life in new tunes. (Fitzgerald, 1925)

The famous scene, now iconic, where Gatsby (Leonardo Di Caprio) toasts
his new acquaintance Nick Carraway (Tobey Maguire), who belongs to
the aristocracy that Gatsby hopes to join in his attempt to win his beloved
Daisy, epitomizes the American Dream and its penchant for ostentation.
Amid fireworks, Gatsby addresses the audience with one arm outstretched
toward the spectator, holding a brimming champagne glass, displaying a
smile that conveys both challenge and confidence in success. This gesture
encapsulates the symbolic power of flaunting possession of an expensive
object. Moving beyond the metaphor of Gatsby and returning to Veblen's
theory (1899), which remains highly relevant in sociological discourse, the
theory explains the artificial world of the Roaring Twenties in the twentieth century. This was a society deeply engaged in economic and social
advancement, obsessed with displaying status and opulence. It simultaneously welcomed the newly wealthy into exclusive circles while rejecting
those deemed pretentious "outsiders." Although Veblen's sociological theory of the "leisure class" referred to his own time, it explains the parable
of the aspirational consumer trends that fueled twentieth-century market
expansion and social development in most economically developed societies, where the highest segment of society is represented by the so-called
"leisure class." The leisure class is made up of those who inherited wealth
and privilege, and, by being free of the burden of producing the goods
they live on, can afford "conspicuous leisure," a condition of *productive
inactivity* spent in wasting time and luxury objects. The leisure class is
that whose members are not required to work, but, at least in the capitalistic societies, do appropriate a surplus produced by those who work, the
working class. Once societies start to produce a surplus, the relationship
between private property and status becomes increasingly important "It
becomes indispensable to accumulate, to acquire property, in order to retain one's good name" (Veblen, 1899, p. 29).

At the core of Veblen's sociological theory of the leisure class, striving
for money and possession of luxury goods becomes a means to display the
newly gained great wealth and social position. The opportunity for social
mobility is encouraged by emulation among other social groups (typical-

ly those placed at an immediately lower standing) creating a system of social norms and reputations more and more associated with appearances, so that display becomes the core of consumption and develops into a normative system that signifies status. Consumption and market gain an unparalleled centrality in the social life of late capitalistic societies, since the appropriation of objects takes the shape of wealth display and consumer preferences are increasingly determined by the position individuals occupy in the social hierarchy.

Within such a social system, the display of possessions and visibly time or money to waste in the absence of having to work becomes the highest sign of privilege whose exclusive holder was the "leisure class."

> The ownership of goods, whether received aggressively by using one's personal exertion or passively with the aid of transmission thru inheritance from others, turns into a traditional foundation of reputability. The possession of wealth, which was at the outset valued honestly as evidence of efficiency, becomes, in famous apprehension, itself a meritorious act. Wealth is now itself intrinsically honourable and confers honour on its possessor. (Veblen, pos. 319 out of 4620 Kindle Edition, p. 29 paper ed. [1899])

To own property means to have status and honor, a position of esteem in this hierarchy that becomes the source of a pecuniary standard of living and pecuniary canons of taste. In this dynamic of status and reputability, inherited wealth confers even more status than wealth that is gained through efficiency. "By a in addition refinement, wealth obtained passively with the aid of transmission from ancestors or different antecedents presently will become even more honorific than wealth received with the aid of the possessor's very own attempt; but this distinction belongs to a later degree in the evolution of the pecuniary culture and may be spoken of in its vicinity" (Veblen, pos. 319 out of 4620, p. 29 paper ed. [1899]).

Veblen identifies two main ways in which individuals display wealth: Through extensive leisure activities and through lavish expenditure on consumption and services. In societies with a higher social mobility, people may be less informed about the leisure activities in which people from higher strata engage, which is why the display of wealth through consumption of goods becomes more important than the display of leisure in more modern and complex societies. When consumption is used as a means to acquire and signal status, it becomes emulative and inevitably "conspicuous." Though during Veblen's era, this phenomenon primarily concerned affluent groups occupying the highest rungs of the social hierarchy, conspicuous consumption was, for Veblen, the pivotal factor destined to shape consumer behavior not only among the wealthy but also across the expanding middle classes.

The social dynamic of consumption described by Veblen suggests, for the first time, the idea of an emulative and aspirational nature of taste, although taste is still viewed as a "scheme of consumption" primarily engaging the upper-wealthy groups who can afford the most exclusive possessions of the richest elites. Moved by "invidious comparison," individuals emulate the consumption patterns of those situated at higher points in the hierarchy and bend their energies to live up to that ideal (Figure 1). The affirmation of one taste over the other totally rests on such a "trickle-down" (Triggs, 2001, p. 107) effect on cultural practices, so that social groups lower down the hierarchy copy those higher up, and through wealth display try to conceal the impression that they are poor.

Figure 1   Veblen's dynamic of "trickle-down" propagation of schemes of consumption among social strata

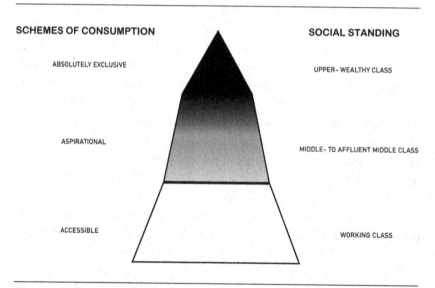

Source: Author's adaptation and personal revisitation of Triggs's (2001) suggestion of "trickle down" propagation of taste.

The result is that the participants of each stratum accept as their perfect of decency the scheme of lifestyles in vogue inside the next better stratum and bend their energies to stay as much as that best. (Veblen, Pos. 960 of 4620 Kindle Edition; paper version p. 52)

The emulative pressure described by Veblen explains the "trickle-down" propagation of taste as a result of the aspirational mechanism of class competition, which has always been the engine of capitalist society since its inception. This mechanism fueled the illusion of "affordable well-being" that would lead to the mass society with its phantom of endless growth and easily accessible luxury. This pressure from below, which has become the essence of consumerism, is often evoked in modern advertising, which relies on the idea of consumeristic rivalry derived from Veblen's theories. This is typically used in advertisement of automotive brands. Expensive cars are often associated with secure and comfortable family transportation (Zestanakis, 2023). For instance, Jeep®, an American brand that has always build its brand reputation of an exclusive car around the subtle but powerful message that "Jeep® isn't just selling a car." In a Jeep® advertisement aired in November 2019, the caption "Not all parents drive a Jeep®" appears in the concluding scene, portraying a child sitting alone in a school classroom. This phrase symbolizes a promise of happiness and love for those who enjoy the exclusive privilege of belonging to a family that owns a Jeep®. This privilege allowed a child to be safely brought to school despite a heavy snowstorm. Initially, this exclusivity seems to isolate the child, as he is the only one who could be chauffeured to school by a Jeep®-owning parent, making him sad, as suggested by the child singing "All by Myself" throughout the journey from home to school. However, by the conclusion of the advertisement, the child discovers that he is not alone, because another girl was also brought to school by another Jeep®-owning family. Sadness turns into sudden joy as the promise of happiness is fulfilled when potential loneliness transforms into a shared sense of belonging to the unique, privileged world of Jeep® owners.

Veblen's theory offers a framework that remains valid for understanding the culture of wealth as an inescapable dimension of societies facing market development and the swift growth of the urban middle class, even in non-Western countries. Conspicuous consumption, as a strategy for social recognition of the ability to acquire surplus wealth, is still widely used as a theoretical framework to understand consumer dynamics in societies such as Russia, China, and India (Global Luxury Survey, 2001). These countries, which lead in luxury consumption, have undergone rapid expansion over the last thirty years, accompanied by the rapid growth of a middle-high class eager to display their newfound patron status (Karpova et al., 2007).

The meaning that luxury goods hold for consumers is fraught with cultural values that differentiate people, but the common element they share is that once you can acquire surplus wealth, you need to enter a symbolic spiral of status display and legitimation, which is exactly what Veblen's theory framed. This concept is brilliantly synthesized by Som (2011):

> The Chinese luxury consumers want mostly outwardly visible and status-driven products which in the luxury parlance is called the "logo strategy." The bigger the logo the more the tendency to show off; more conspicuously demonstrate the products can be consumed. The Indian luxury consumers are different - they are more conscious and are probably searching to customize their needs. Thus, what the Chinese consumers would want today is not what the Indian consumers would want today. Similarly, in Russia, the consumers expect luxury products to have a balance between tradition, modesty, and wealth. And interestingly, Russian consumers usually have been seen to buy goods that have much higher prices than they are ordinarily sold at because they like to show off that they can spend that amount of money for a valuable product. Thus concluding, consumers in these countries have become more and more aware and conscious of not only quality but also status.

"Conspicuous consumption" inevitably brings about "conspicuous waste." Indeed, the element common to all forms of conspicuous consumption is waste. Conspicuous consumers are those who buy expensive items to display wealth and income rather than to cover the real needs of the consumer. But this search for status is never ending and what at a certain time may confer status, once it is acquired by all, confers no status anymore and pushes to find new "honorific" items of consumption.

"From the foregoing survey of the growth of conspicuous amusement and intake, it appears that the utility of both alike for the functions of reputability lies inside the detail of waste that is commonplace to both. In the only case it's far a waste of effort and time, inside the different it is a waste of products. Both are techniques of demonstrating the possession of wealth, and the 2 are conventionally familiar as equivalents (Veblen, Pos. 977 out of 4620 Kindle Edition; p. 53 paper edition)."

Veblen's account of the "irrational but strategic" dynamic of consumption in late capitalistic society represents a powerful critique of the neoclassical theory of consumption (typical of early capitalism) – according to which the individual only aspired to maximize the utility of consumed goods according to exogenous preferences – and provides the first authentic sociological theorization of consumption.

Let's think about some definitions that entered the economic language and are still current today, such as "Veblen goods," an expression used to explain the economic dynamic of price and social desirability of goods determined by the irrational relationship with objects that consumers establish outside the boundaries of mere income effect.

A Veblen good is a good with an added symbolic value: a "snob value," which "shows off" status. Veblen goods designate luxury or extremely expensive products, whose value only relies upon their power to confer "honorific wealth." They function as positional goods: Products people buy because of their status symbol value, mainly owing to their limited supply, and, in some cases, to their rarity, and, just because of this, to convey a high relative standing within society. They include rare goods, such as collectibles that are deemed priceless because of their rarity and can reach a crazy price at auctions, brand-name goods, luxury goods, in general all those goods affected by the so called "Veblen effect," according to which the demand of a good increases when the price of that good rises, a behavior that goes against the flow of common sense and common buying behavior.

In the mass-consumption society, in which we still live, conspicuous consumption remains a growing factor in the economics of high-demand goods, such as smartphones. The iPhone represents a paradigmatic example of a positional good. When high-priced, high-end super-premium models are launched, demand surges due to the Veblen effect, which suggests that the perception of a super-premium product elevates its desirability among consumers, who feel themselves pushed to the stratosphere. Considering the huge array of similar goods on the market and their rapid obsolescence, this seems the most credible interpretation, though corporate executives deny this, attributing the trend less to the quest for a status symbol and more to the awareness that they are buying the best smartphone in the world (The Wall Street Journal, 2017).

In the field of food, such a Veblen dynamic has been represented by the development and worldwide success of French *Haute Cuisine*, an ideal of "refined food" that since its appearance has always conjured up social contrasts. Indeed "refined food," best known as "fine food" has always been a means to convey the superiority of upper classes, and increasing refinement in cookery as in manners is the sign of a relentless, "from below" pressure to keep social distances from ascending social groups, and to modernization.

A food item that has come to represent a "Veblen good" is wine. Wine becomes a fine luxury good when, having become an exclusive and pricey consumer product, it also gains value as a legitimate investment asset. This transformation of wine into a conspicuous product is part of the global expansion of the wine industry, especially in developing countries such as China and India, where wine is associated with the pursuit of status and reputation by a rapidly growing urban upper-middle class embracing a Western and modern lifestyle. Wine production, as an economic activity yielding profits, has attracted a growing number of investors at different scales, from celebrities and individual investors to private equity funds worldwide (Overton and Banks, 2015). As explained on the emblematic fine wine trade website veblenwine.com, by the end of the 1980s, fine wine had already consistently outperformed global equities. Since the 2000s, investment indexes have been specifically created for the fine wine market. A bottle of Chianti that appreciates over time and equates to an investment is no longer thought of for consumption but becomes a collector's fetish, a status symbol, and a positional good. Whether they are vintage champagnes or aging reds sold *en primeur*, that is, months or years before being marketed, a segment of fine wine is destined to become a precious asset for collectors, often auctioned at high prices. Especially in times of crisis, the search for fine bottles has become a safe haven asset, like gold (Il Sole 24 Ore, 2022). Dominating the trading of fine wines are those that evoke rarity, such as Burgundy or Champagne, where the scarcity of harvests in the Côte d'Or has driven up prices. These wines often have, or just claim to have, a unique tie to a terroir – a marketing concept denoting the physical (geology, climate) and cultural characteristics of a place – which imbue the wine with special qualities. These characteristics are often branded by geographic indication labels of origin as a form of intellectual property, making investing in a wine essentially an investment in a place (Overton and Murray, 2016). In Italy, for the past thirty years, wines associated with regions like Tuscany (which holds 50% of the fine wine luxury market) and Piedmont with Barolo have dominated. There is a broad literature (Kung, 2008; West, 2008; Levine, 2012; Overton and Banks, 2015) evidencing a process of branding of places going along with the aestheticization of wine and its glorification as an exclusive asset created (and not merely produced) by the unique gesture of the producer seen as an artist. One example is the "Triple A" movement ("Agricoltori, Artigiani, Artisti"), founded in Italy in 2001 by the liquor entrepreneur Luca Gargano. The third "A" in the "Triple A" protocol alludes to "the artistic sensitivity of a producer who, respecting their work and ideas, can create a great wine that enhances the characteristics of the territory and the grape variety."[2] On the other hand, consider the reverse of this phenomenon, where real artists or celebrities, such as Gérard Depardieu, Madonna, Cliff Richard, and others became producers motivated by status-seeking rather than pure profit maximization. An emblematic case is Antonio Banderas, who declared that "Making wine is creating art" (Overton and Banks, 2015, p. 473).

At the end, Veblen tells us that, if the trickle-down effect on taste differentiation is the result of the competitive rampant bourgeois society, so that lower strata tend to emulate the tastes and behavior of those on a higher tier, the pressure to change and embrace new tastes is always the result of a push from below by groups of outsiders that aspire to enter the restricted circles of the élites. Once the tastes of the élites become accessible to the middle and lower classes, their exclusivity and status signaling diminish. New positional goods, behaviors, or experiences that are out of reach for the lower classes then take the stage.

Conspicuous consumption, characterized by a taste for extravagance and a relentless pursuit of status displays, appeals to emulative aspirations and excessive consumption, epitomizing the wasteful and unsustainable nature of predatory consumerism. This aspect is often masked by the prevailing notion that a luxury item, which is also a positional good, is also of high product quality based on most innovative and aware use of technology, as opposed to "fast" products which are standardized and low cost. In fact, market insights highlight that luxury brands play an important role in moving the broader fashion industry toward an en-

---

[2] https://www.triplea.it/it/movimento/manifesto-produttori-vino-triple-a-8.html.

vironmentally responsible, circular economy (Deloitte, 2023). However, as we have read in the previous pages, beyond the quality standard and method of production, the logic of waste is intrinsic to Veblen's concept, where consumption itself was the source of pleasure for an idle and non-productive class, whose idleness and nonproductivity were the distinctive marks of privilege.

3.1.1 *Limits and criticism of the theory of conspicuous consumption*

Conspicuous consumption embodies the ideal of a predatory capitalism based on the illusion of endless growth, but is no longer compatible with the values of the Eco-Anthropocene.

Conspicuous consumption embodies the consumeristic ideal of a society pursuing endless economic growth, and indeed it is a constant that repeats in the social dynamics of economic growth. Nevertheless, conspicuous consumption also poses a social limit to growth. As noted by Hirsch himself (1976), positional goods are inherently limited in their availability, and the value of their consumption is predicated upon a restricted number of consumers. In times of ecological crisis and sustainable development, ecological limits to conspicuous consumption add to the social ones. Let's consider the impact of conspicuous consumption in some emerging market economies, where the desire to display newly gained social status coexists with persistent traditional food habits and beliefs. In Far Eastern countries such as Vietnam and certain parts of China, the demand for pangolin meat or tiger bone wine, driven by the pursuit of rarity and status (Menon et al., 2019), is leading to the extinction of these wild animal species. The possession of these items plays a significant social role, signaling wealth or social status. However, the consequences of this trade, largely confined to the realms of illegality, have proven to be detrimental not only to the ecosystem but also to health. Pangolins have been shown to be highly vulnerable to COVID-19 infection (Deng et al., 2024), and their gathering with other wild animal meats under the same roof at the wet market in Wuhan has been identified as the likely primary cause of the COVID-19 spillover and pandemic outbreak (Brüssow, 2023).

Though utopian may seem, a vision outlining a shift away from the endless growth paradigm, sobriety, minimalism, and reuse have become predicaments of degrowth and parts of a sustainable societal and economic framework. In the wake of Baudrillard's (1998) denunciation of consumer society's dedication to growth driven by its insatiable desire for goods that serve not only practical purposes but also as symbols, Serge Latouche in his book "Farewell to Growth" (2010) advocates degrowth, which entails:

> the systematic and ambitious articulation of eight inter-dependent changes that reinforces one-another [...] and that can be synthetized into a virtuous circle of eight 'Rs': re-evaluate, reconceptualize, relocate, restructure, redistribute, reduce, reuse, and recycle. These eight interdependent goals can trigger a process of de-growth that will be serene, convivial and sustainable. (Latouche, 2010, p. 33)

The eight "Rs" are the new pillars of circular economy and responsible consumption and production paradigm. According to Sustainable Development Goal 12 set by the UN Agenda, this paradigm calls for a substantial reduction in waste generation through prevention, reduction, recycling, and reuse by 2030.[3]

3.1.1.1 Conspicuous consumption only refers to luxury goods

According to this theory, the pacesetters of emerging trends in consumption are the élites, who trigger an emulative mechanism of consumption according to a trickle-down effect from the top of the social hierarchy to the bottom; the emerging trends in consumption are ruled by a concentration on some goods, namely, expensive and luxury goods. Although the luxury market, in all its forms, appears to be recession-proof (Deloitte, 2023), and global market insights forecast a steady 2–4% growth in the luxury fashion in 2024,[4] also aided by artificial intelligence, not all consumption can be explained in terms of "emulation." Emulation is a social behavior that can be applied to goods likely to become "fashionable," but in some cases, the availability of certain goods simply results

---

[3] See: https://sdgs.un.org/goals/goal12#targets_and_indicator (accessed on 24/06/2024).

[4] See: https://www.mckinsey.com/industries/retail/our-insights/state-of-fashion (accessed on 23/06/2024).

from improving life conditions and demographic growth, especially in urban contexts.

3.1.1.2 In cultural omnivores' times, people consume conspicuously not only to display their wealth but also status

Even when emulative mechanisms are at stake, the one-directional focus on the transmission of tastes and preferences from the top-down of the social hierarchy results too narrow. Let's take the case of jeans, a resistant long-wearing item of the working class, whose success as a mass-produced item of consumption did not take place because of the behavior of the upper classes. Blue jeans seem to prove that the "trickle-up" dynamic of consumption may be as important as "trickle down" ones theorized by conspicuous consumption.

Situations like these typically happen during periods of economic depression or crisis, when, given the hardships experienced by those at the bottom of the social hierarchy, flaunting wealth becomes less acceptable. Typically, in this case, the rich turn their consumption choices into less ostentatious behaviors and pecuniary availability is channeled toward social activities and charity-related initiatives. Or, this happens when redundancy and excessiveness dominate the stylistic expressions of the emerging lower and middle bourgeois classes, and higher social echelons deliberately reject these norms in favor of a unique aesthetic. This shift heralds a preference for the "natural," the "simple," and the "rough," embodying a cultural framework that emphasizes relative simplicity in objects. This frankness of the object must not be confused with inconspicuousness, as it isn't inherently natural but rather a semiotic manipulation of consumer goods. These goods remain part of a "social standing code," contrasting with the baroque pretensions of the lower and middle bourgeoisie. Thus, qualities of essentiality and values such as "sincerity," "authenticity," and "simplicity" – evident in minimalist decor, a return to natural foods, and the aestheticization of natural landscapes, as in the case of "triple A" wine – function as social markers expressed in cultural rather than material terms.

3.1.1.3 In postmodern times, consumer behavior is shaped by lifestyles rather than class positions

The conspicuous production of wine exemplifies the amplification of the concept of locality as a branding strategy, often symbolized by the over-used concept of *terroir*, which serves marketing more than the intrinsic characteristics of the wine. While the land – with its unique features such as rainfall, temperature, aspect, slope, soils, and geology – is integral to winemaking and is supposed to shape the structural and sensory qualities of the final product, investing in land to secure grape provenance through a system of labels and certifications emphasizing geographical origin plays a pivotal role in transforming land into the cultural and economic construct of *terroir*. The significance of a place is increasingly emphasized through claims of origin denomination and geographic indications, as well as organic production or ethical labor practices, which serve as distinctive elements contributing to the exclusive quality of a product. These factors thereby emerge as pivotal aspects of wine brands, appealing to affluent consumers not only for signaling wealth or a collector's passion but also for demonstrating discernment and consciousness. This construct carries profound sociological implications, influencing evolving patterns of consumer behavior. Specifically, it involves the progressive internalization of material differences, transforming the possession of objects to exhibit into *dispositional* skills of cultural classification. These shifts in consumer attitudes toward products prompt a corresponding evolution in sociological theories that best frame these changing behaviors.

This is the key point marking the shift from Veblen's status-seeking tradition of class dynamics of consumption to Bourdieu's (1984 [1979]) broader interest in expressive processes of class-based divisions, revealing an influence of Baudrillard's (1998 [1970]) and, more generally, semiotic ideas of consumption as a signification system and taste as a language. The rarity of the product and its unique connection to the territory, as intrinsic qualifications of objects that also determine their market position – such as fine wine or white truffle, another positional good – increasingly combine with subjective skills to acknowledge and convey the intrinsic relationships between objects. This contributes to the status-signaling symbolic power of possessing those objects, where nuances of social identity are conveyed by the suggested degree of familiarity with them.

3.2   The distinctive role of taste in consumption

The French sociologist Pierre Bourdieu (1930–2002) distinguished himself for his consistent focus in his analysis on cultural patterns as manifestations of persistent inequalities and class domination, becoming one of the most influential cultural sociologists in late-modern society, particularly in the field of consumption. In his theory of taste as a primary factor of social distinction, Bourdieu offers a contemporary development of the theory of conspicuous consumption, surpassing certain limitations inherent in aspects of Veblen's framework. His monumental work "Distinction: A Social Critique of the Judgement of Taste" (1984 [1979]) is part of his broader theory of cultural reproduction of social inequalities in the societies stratified on the basis of a class system, a theory through which he especially investigates the competitive dimension of taste, and takes up issues of stratification mainly in terms of lifestyles and habits.

Like Veblen (1899), but also Baudrillard (1998, [orig. 1970]) and even Douglas and Isherwood (1979), Bourdieu conceptualizes consumption as a cultural practice operating within a system of markings encoding social differences. Like Veblen, Bourdieu's analysis of consumption clearly assigns to consumer goods the function of objectifying and legitimizing class differences and their distinctive relationships. However, Bourdieu's model is more flexible than Veblen's, as it shifts attention from the characteristics of objects conferring status to the tastes and propensities of subjects conferring meaning in terms of status when they relate to those objects. This shift accounts for social complexity and the influence of semiotic understanding of cultural practices, including taste, within a system of representations, paving the way for omnivorous cultural tastes.

Bourdieu provides a further developed and updated concept of conspicuous consumption, by enhancing the cultural and symbolic dimensions intrinsic in consumer behaviors, as well as the social complexity underlying people's habituses and manifest tastes. According to his theory,

> Tastes function as markers of 'class'. The manner in which culture has been acquired lives on in the manner of using it. (Bourdieu, 1984, p. 2)

For the first time, the entire spectrum of internalized dimensions of taste, rather than merely the externalized objects of purchase, is analyzed as a field of sociological investigation. Taste is not only the relatively stable set of preferences for a certain class of objects but also the ability to engage in aesthetic judgment regarding those objects. It serves as a marker for differentiation within economic hierarchies but also within cultural stratification, as it depends on a certain level of cultural competency: "to see (voir) is a function of knowledge (savoir)" (Bourdieu, 1984, p. 2).

This analysis explores taste as a complex sociocultural category that transforms the naïve exhibitionism of "conspicuous consumption" into the unique capacity for the pure gaze and the quasi-creative power of the connoisseur, a distinction that appears to be inscribed in individuals rather than in objects. To continue using the cinematographic metaphor, we can say that this shift is from the naïve exhibitionism of Gatsby to the skillful gaze of Miles, the failed, depressed novelist but serious-leisure wine lover protagonist of the movie *Sideways* (2004).[5] The movie is an American comedy-drama road film that tells the story of two friends in their forties: Miles (Paul Giamatti), a depressed teacher and unsuccessful writer but a good wine lover, and Jack (Thomas Haden Church), a washed-up actor and womanizer. They embark on a week-long road trip to Santa Barbara County wine country to celebrate Jack's last week as a single man before his wedding. During this journey through the vineyards and wineries of California, the wine lover is determined to introduce his friend to the world of wine before the week is out. The other is primarily interested in enjoying his last week as a bachelor, but nevertheless gives in to his friend's passion, which often leads to comic effects, as the scene of the wine tasting, where Miles celebrates the flavorful characteristics of a wine to his friend Jack. This scene shows the two protagonists stopping at a winery and taste a special wine. The scene shows Miles profoundly concentrated on the wine tasting, with eyes closed, nose close to the glass, and finger closing the ear, to capture, appreciate and tell his friend the "secret," sensory perceptible qualities of the wine. In this scene, consumption is portrayed not just as an economic act but also as a meaningful sequence of gestures.

Comparing this image of Miles and Jack to the one of *The Great Gatsby*, we can visually grasp two dynamics of taste at stake. In the above referred scene, the parvenu Gatsby is iconically portrayed in the act of in-

---

[5] Based on the eponymous novel by Rex Pickett, "Sideways" is a 2004 USA comedy-drama movie directed by Alexander Payne, produced by Michael London, and distributed by Fox Searchlight Pictures (Running time: 127').

troducing himself and, while doing so, he addresses the audience with an outstretched arm, holding a glass of champagne as a sign of his affluence. His consumption posture is characterized by exhibitionistic gestures that display objects outwardly, distancing them from himself toward others. This scene exemplifies Veblen's taste dynamic, which is based on the "ostentatious" display of status and relies entirely on the possession of luxury goods as a sign of material wealth.

By contrast, the wine tasting scene in *Sideways* lingers on the well-educated middle-class protagonist, Miles, the "connoisseur," as he draws the distinctive object, a glass of wine, closer to himself to gaze at, smell, describe, and finally sip. This inwardly oriented movement reflects a sort of internalization of the relationship with the object, transforming it into a classificatory skill, an inclination, a distinctive taste that, even when exhibited to others, is inseparable from the subject who has appropriated it. This act cannot be limited to the mere display of economic energy; it also demonstrates other subjective, internalized endowments that include knowledge, experience, habitus refinement, and the availability of social opportunities where this knowledge can be acquired, trained, and displayed.

Sideways is a good example of the development of conspicuous consumption into a distinctive engagement with taste. The influential consumer is no longer the naive exhibitionist like Gatsby but the skillful connoisseur like Miles. This transformation is also paradigmatically cast in the world of wine, proving not by chance to have remarkable repercussions not only on conspicuous wine consumption but also on conspicuous production. Throughout the film, Miles shows a great fondness for the red wine variety Pinot Noir in particular, while disparaging Merlot. Following the film's release in the US in October 2004, sales of Merlot fell by 2%, while sales of Pinot Noir rose by 16%. A similar trend was observed in British wine shops. After the unexpected success of the film, the author of the *Sideways* novel, Rex Pickett, released his own Pinot Noir called "Le Plus Ultra." Many years later, in 2020, as the movie became a cult favorite among wine lovers, he released another Pinot Noir named "Sideways."[6]

---

[6] Winediplomats (January 9, 2021). *Review & Interview with Rex Pickett about his Sideways Pinot Noir – The Wine Diplomats*. The Wine Diplomats. https://winediplomats.com/review-interview-with-rex-pickett-about-his-sideways-pinot-noir/ (accessed on 03/07/2024).

These two movies exemplify the central role of taste within the evolving emulative social dynamics of late-modern, omnivorous consumer society – a concept Bourdieu pioneeringly captured and framed in his cutting-edge sociological theory of "distinction," which remains relevant today with contemporary adaptations. *Taste operates as a system of manifested preferences guiding practical choices and affirming practical differences* (Bourdieu, 1984, p. 6). These preferences serve dual purposes: *They act as fences, delineating boundaries and expressing distaste*, while also functioning *as bridges that facilitate the discovery of commonalities*, thus reflecting evolving identities in the process of social mobility. Taste is wholly shaped by *status competition* which characterizes the struggle within a well-defined social space. *Good taste*, that actually emulates or corresponds to *legitimate taste*, is a mark of distinction, in the double sense of *setting apart from*, and *conferring honor to* those who claim to possess it.

Taste confers honor not simply because it is a signal of economic wealth, but rather because it works as an expression of cultural wealth and refinement (*savoir faire*). Taste refinement is part of a process of acquiring the legitimate taste that distinguishes the upper classes. This dynamic is not at all new in the sociological understanding of food consumption. Taste refinement and the introduction of a sense of measurement and self-control over the "gargantuan appetite" of the aristocracy as part of a civilizing process in court society, used as a distinctive strategy once the food supply became available to the lower classes, were first thematized by Norbert Elias (1978/1983 [1939]; 1983 [1969]). This theme was later revisited by Mennell et al. (1992), emphasizing the symbolic side of this process of differentiation and criticizing Bourdieu's conceptualization of habitus as too deterministic. Indeed, Bourdieu recognizes that food taste, understood as the capability to engage in judgment about one's own food practices and consumption choices, plays a unique role as a marker of social status and, to a certain extent, cultural reproduction: The higher this capability, the more refinement is demonstrated, bringing one closer to the legitimate taste. With this study, Bourdieu developed a theory that would become a milestone in sociological theories of social action applied to consumption. Consumption is linked to its sociocultural and communicative device – taste – which is refinable as part of a social mobility process where individuals emulate the lifestyles of the fractions of their class status immediately above them. However, taste is less ephemeral and self-determined than one might imagine, as it relies on habitus,

a persistent socially shaped disposition that begins forming in the early
stages of socialization and finds its simulacrum of reproduction in legitimate taste.

We can still find powerful cinematographic representation of this social dynamics of class differences and cultural elitism expressed through
culinary taste rivalry. Let's think of the 2014 successful film "The Hundred-Foot Journey"[7] telling the story of the rivalry between a migrant
Indian family who opens a restaurant in a quaint French village, just
across the street from a Michelin-starred French restaurant. Probably
beyond its intentions, the film shows well how, the rivalry between the
ethnically different culinary tastes and styles of two restaurants actually
hides broader and deeper themes of class differences and cultural elitism. The rich and flavorful Indian cuisine, representing in the portrayed
cultural context a more humble and exotic culinary tradition, challenges
and questions the Michelin-starred French restaurant, which epitomizes
haute cuisine and the culinary sophistication of its tradition, symbolizing
upper-class taste and refinement. The famous window scene, where the
two protagonists – the man running the Indian restaurant (Omi Pur) and
the highbrow French woman (Helen Mirren) running the starred restaurant and looking down at him standing on the street – argue about their
different culinary tastes and the woman advocates "classical taste." The
woman asserts that "classical" derives from "class," emphasizing that in
her restaurant they "cook with class" and the Indian's young son training
at her restaurant will "learn to cook with class." This is a very dense scene,
evoking what Bourdieu would call "legitimate taste" and highlighting
how, in this process of acculturation, food can be a powerful symbol not
only of cultural identity but also of social status. Behind the restaurants'
efforts to assert their culinary superiority in the name of authenticity lies
a deeper motive: The French woman's defense of social status against
the perceived pressure from below, represented by migrants "invading" a
privileged field and challenging elite legitimate taste. At the end, a trickle-round dynamic is shown in the movie when the Indian man with a
talent for cooking, after receiving classical French cuisine training, becomes a chef at the lady's renowned Michelin restaurant. Conversely, this

---

[7] *The Hundred-Foot Journey* is a 2014 USA American comedy-drama film directed by Lasse Hallström, adapted from Richard C. Morais' 2010 novel of the
same name and distributed by Disney (Running time: 155').

process of taste refinement is accompanied by gastronomic contamination brought by his informally gained culinary knowledge. This evolves into a unique French-Indian fusion, resulting in the restaurant being awarded a second Michelin star. Ultimately, this process is not only cultural (culinary contamination) but also one of social distinction – a new legitimate taste emerging from the tastes of the lower classes, which the higher classes appropriate and legitimize through a process of refinement.

In this story, we see an element introduced by Bourdieu's theory: The dynamic of taste propagation becomes "trickle-round" (Triggs, 2001, p. 107). In the previous chapter, we discussed the case of blue jeans transitioning from a working-class item to a consumption object among higher classes and later becoming popular across all social classes. This shift occurred because they symbolized the casual, easy-going, and mobile living habits associated with modern urban lifestyles. Although in Veblen's analysis of emulative consumption we find precursor concepts like "schemes of life" and "styles of fashion," there is no explicit consideration of "lifestyles," which is a relatively new concept further investigated by Bourdieu. In Bourdieu's theory of distinction, the dynamic of taste differentiation diverges from Veblen's. Taste integrates structure (the collective social factors shaping human behavior) and agency (individual willingness and motivation to act, independent of social constraints), contributing to the outline of lifestyles as spheres of practices where both cultural and socially shaped factors come into play. Veblen views the propagation of these schemes of life as a one-way, trickle-down, vertical process, while Bourdieu, by introducing the concept of habitus as a set of dispositions fed by both economic and cultural capital, provides a model in which lifestyles, though mainly driven by pressure from below, can vary horizontally, even cutting across the social hierarchy.

In the wake of Veblen, Bourdieu's analysis keeps its focus on the "drive from below" shaping evolving tastes of social classes during processes of social mobility, expanding his gaze to include the lower classes in mass-consumption societies. However, he also introduces a new focus on the upper class's highbrow impulse to adopt new tastes in response to this "pressure from below," distinguishing themselves from "new money" by often appropriating less ostentatious consumption styles typically associated with lower classes. This impulse leans on a culturally, and not only economically, distinctive use of resources. By identifying these dynamics as manifestations of proper lifestyles in terms of both habitus and taste, Bourdieu exposes the hypocritical and snobbish nature of the upper-middle class, where two orders – and no longer just one – of personal resources are in play: Economic and cultural. This complicates the purely vertical direction of taste propagation identified by Veblen, while maintaining the basic emulative and socially distinctive nature of desire that drives consumption. Indeed, Bourdieu also identifies a taste of popular culture and recognizes it as a more genuine form of bottom-up resistance by the lower classes against the tastes of those higher in the social hierarchy, thereby predicting the eventual appropriation of popular culture by the upper classes.

Remaining in the sphere of food consumption, there are many examples of this "trickle-round" dynamic of social pressure toward partly emulative, but mostly distinctive, appropriation of the tastes and consumption patterns of nearby classes. The identification of popular taste and the presence of symbolic, cultural elements in the process of taste propagation make the "trickle-round" dynamic described by Triggs even more complex. This complexity arises not only due to the mediation of the cultural and symbolic capital of the middle classes but also because a direct exchange between popular taste and the upper classes may occur as part of a "gentrification" of taste (Sbicca, 2018), especially when legitimate taste is no longer exclusively distinctive of the élites. This process involves the expropriation and colonization of taste from the popular classes, often manifesting through forms of "green gentrification" affecting their areas and food-related cultures.

As part of this "more than trickle-round" appropriation of tastes, we have seen how a return to nature and the hidden world of peasant culture characterizes a new formula of high-end wine production known as "Triple A." This formula is intended for niche consumption and embodies a new ostentatious display of knowledge and awareness – not just economic availability – for well-educated and affluent wine lovers who reject more conventional and unsustainable urban styles. Clearly, this wine is not accessible to the lower classes, who, perhaps to display their achieved better-off lifestyle, will opt for more versatile and economically accessible wines, such as prosecco or rosé, which are particularly suitable, for example, for mixology, leisure consumption, and typically urban sociability, which, at least in the initial stages, characterizes the *nouveaux riches*. Market insights show that these products are also undergoing a process of marketing "aestheticization," which moves them beyond fashion, associating them with a narrative that transforms them from being seen as inferior reds or bland wines to versatile expressions of grape varieties with great minerality and freshness or with *terroirs* (Pazzano, 2022). These wines become symbols of a region or the ideal pairing for light dishes, such as vegetables, white meats, and raw fish, reflecting the dietary style of the upper-middle classes. This process has turned rosé wine into one of the preferred products for private equity investors (Huyghe, 2023). The entry into the financial sector transforms it into a form of conspicuous production (Cole, 2021) – consider the so-called "celebrity rosés" produced by Brad Pitt, John Legend, Cameron Diaz, Sarah Jessica Parker, and Post Malone (Mazzeo, 2023) – and a product for conspicuous consumption, such as the magnificent rosés of famous Champagne brands. Thus, the trickle-round model will be self-perpetuating (Figure 2).

Figure 2 "More than trickle round" model of taste propagation in the theory of distinction

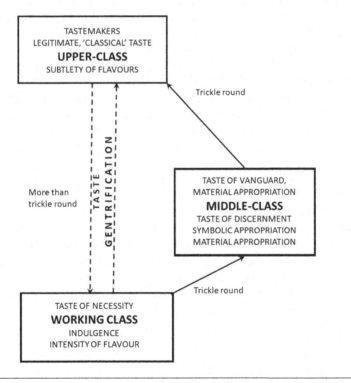

Source: Author's revision of "trickle round" model by Triggs (2001).

3.3   The role of habitus in the taste propagation and cultural reproduction

The real step beyond Veblen's theory, which endows the distinction theory with subtleties and more hidden aspects of socially shaped drives to
consumption, is the introduction of the concept of habitus. Habitus is a
central concept in Bourdieu's theory of social practice and, together with
the concept of legitimate taste, makes his theory a powerful sociological
understanding of cultural reproduction.

*Bourdieu introduces the concept of habitus and cultural capital to interpret
individual tastes and propensities as accumulated stocks of knowledge or of advantage.* Habitus is "a socially constituted system of dispositions orienting thoughts, perceptions, expressions, and actions" (Bourdieu, 1984).
This concept refers to the ingrained perspectives, experiences, and *pre-
dispositions that individuals share with others in similar social positions.* As
a mixture of formally and informally gained acquisitions, structured by
the social environment (i.e., legitimate within the social group individuals belong to or come from), and structuring it in return by unreflex-
ively informing taste, habitus reiterates, consolidates, and reproduces
these acquisitions. *Habitus represents internalized cultural capital,* namely,
socially constituted practical schemes that dispose individuals to prefer
some objects and to make certain choices of consumption similar to those
made by his/her own group. *By becoming manifest in attitudes, preferences,
passions, and elective consumption choices – all that we call taste – provides
information about how that capital was acquired.* Through this function,
habitus retranslates the (relatively) homogeneous conditions of existence
of a class into a particular lifestyle (1984, p. 208). This is the generative
formula of taste as a marker of "class."

Since *habitus* is embedded in class position, choices and tastes are not
only a matter of individual personality and personal inclination but also
and mostly of class differences in behavior. It incorporates the agency of
individuals in the context of a structural process of social determinism
and that becomes manifest through tastes and through a whole of the
unintended classificatory devices totally embedded in the cultural codes
of a field or a society and its contradictory drives. Habitus equips agents
with a practical sense to understand, navigate, and act within a given
field, since it speaks for the embodied objective structures of a field or
any social environment. Just because of this, habitus represents the ring

that inextricably connects structure and agency and to such an extent it is part of the gear of "the circuit of reproduction." It represents a brake on the potential of taste and lifestyles to subvert the accepted distribution of capitals and resources within a field. However, precisely because of this, it serves a highly revealing function: It disguises the advantage gained from exposure to a rich language or being raised in cultured environments, making privileged children appear "naturally endowed" with talent rather than beneficiaries of acquired advantages. But habitus also explains the cultural force that pushes people to buy, for instance, expensive garments that are not immediately visible, such as underwear and kitchen utensils, proves that consumption is postulated not simply as a fully conscious ostentation of pecuniary power, but rather as a standard of decency that exerts social pressure on behavior.

However, habitus largely relies on *doxa* (or *doxic* beliefs), which is the unreflexive internalization of knowledge considered valuable and reliable within a field. Habitus represents a structure of action that reconciles the determinism of external social forces, cultural ethos, and individual agency. However, given the conservative and conformist nature of *doxa* (Bourdieu and Wacquant, 1992, p. 72), habitus functions more in cultural reproduction than in subversion. Thus, if one is to understand the logic of practice behind a given field in a given social context, it is imperative to carefully examine not only the nature of practices but also how their organization serves specific values or classificatory systems, which are incorporated into individuals' habitues. Recent studies applying Bourdieu's theory of distinction to the ongoing reconfiguration of tourism's field of taste within a context of culinary celebrification capture transitions in habitus and points of break within cultural reproduction (Stringfellow et al., 2013).

3.4   Consumer lifestyles as a strategy of social distinction

The way a person's living room is furnished, how they spend their holidays and leisure time, the voluntary associations to which they belong, and their usual choice of restaurants are parts of their lifestyle that convey status and the position they occupy on the social ladder. Thanks to Bourdieu's famous work *Distinction* (1984 [1979]), we can recognize consumption as the manifest side of the symbolic competition undertaken by individuals occupying different locations in the class structure to draw symbolic boundaries between different class fractions. Specifically, he had us regard lifestyles as socially ranked, organized manifestations of taste in the form of consumer priorities and tendencies inherent to specific groups. Taste for haute cuisine or for hearty food in the field of gastronomy, for an antique collection or for Ikea supplies in the field of furniture or fashion, for a conventional sparkling wine or for a biodynamic one, etc., are not simply preferences, but elements of socially ranked lifestyles standing in a hierarchical relation to one another.

The appropriation of the most "distinguished" objects or practices within specific fields as part of a status-asserting competition, is what Bourdieu calls "distinction." It is where the dominant class acts as the "taste-maker," being the carrier of legitimate taste. Bourdieu explicitly takes up Weber's well-known account of "class" and "stand," the latter interpreted as a "status group": The honor and reputation attached to people occupying a certain stand, not only as a consequence of their economic capacity. Bourdieu considers social class a multidimensional construct and interprets Weber's contrast between class and status in terms of a distinction between the material (or "economic") and the symbolic (or "prestige"). This is why social struggle is not only waged at the economic level but also at the level of tastes. Taste emerges from and is employed in struggles for social recognition and status.

3.5 Distinction always takes place within fields as an exchange of capitals

Social competition doesn't take place in a void but in the social space. The social space, in turn – and the whole of the practices taking place within it – is not merely a broad amalgam of elements, whether they are cultural values such as religion, ethnicity, symbols, language, principles, and beliefs, or structural factors such as class, gender, age, and income. These elements are organized in the social space to form fields, which are spatial arenas where people maneuver and compete for desirable resources. Fields are structured spaces of agency where individuals' free actions, based on their inner habituses and assets, gain relevance and are delimited by specific external rules.

A field is, therefore, not at all an innocent or neutral space; it is a structured space of positions, a relational ambit of forces operating upon those acting within it. At the same time, it is an ambit where social agents struggle to preserve or transform the distribution of resources. Access to a field is, therefore, never "free"; it is subject to the possession of endowments relevant to the field, that is, material and immaterial assets that are valuable as long as they can be exchanged for other assets to gain positions within the field.

The initial assets, practices, and productions put into the field by individuals are evaluated according to the rules and criteria functioning within that particular domain of activity. *The position that agents occupy in a field depends on the volume and structure of their assets valued as capital.* Capital is not simply assets, but resources that can be strategically exchanged within the field to gain advantages. Generally speaking, some assets are more valued than others and gain relevance according to the particular field. Fields are governed by distinct systems of norms. Different fields have different logics that make various forms of capital more or less relevant in each 'market.' The field is indeed a distinctive social microcosm characterized by its own system of practices, rules, forms of authority, and standards of evaluation (Bourdieu and Wacquant, 1992, pp. 101–102).

Beyond formal rules and their standards, there is another set of rules governing fields related to informally shared knowledge, mainly internalized through practice, which Bourdieu calls *doxa*. *Doxa* is a set of internalized beliefs that affect agents' actions at a pre-reflexive level, generally at the level of perception. It is not a "state of mind" nor does it represent an arbitrary adherence to instituted dogmas and doctrines ("beliefs"). Rather, a *doxic* belief is a state of the body, relying on the immediate adherence in practice between a *habitus* and the conventions of the field to which it is attuned.

Doxa operates at a pre-reflexive level, creating the preverbal, taken-for-granted world that forms the basis of any practical sense and endows individuals with routine know-how. It underpins what Bourdieu calls "the logic of practice," or "the universe of the undiscussed," characterized by unquestioned aspects of practice legitimized by doxa within social orders. *Doxa* represents the bodily foundation of social orders that govern fields, relating to habitus, and stands in opposition to opinion, which emerges from mental elaborations within "the universe of discourse." *Doxa* represents the most radical form of acceptance of the world and the most absolute form of conservatism. This prereflexive acceptance, rooted in a fundamental belief in the immediacy of world-of-life structures, epitomizes ultimate conformism (Bourdieu and Wacquant, 1992, p. 72).

It is the field, with its formal and informal rules, that decides the relevance of individual endowments, turning them into exchangeable capital. Capital is a central concept in Bourdieu's theory. He builds on Karl Marx's work on economic capital but extends it significantly by theorizing the existence of multiple forms of capital – economic, cultural, symbolic, and social – circulating across social fields and at stake in the social competition among classes and class fractions. In Bourdieu's theory of distinction, the concept of capital does not simply refer to economic resources; it is a multidimensional asset that functions in "reproduction," meaning the forms of unequal transmission of power in society. And, as seen before, habitus – the internalized acquisition of resources available in the contexts where individuals grow up – is the mechanism of cultural reproduction.

Unlike Marx, Bourdieu's concept of reproduction encompasses not only the unequal distribution of material wealth due to class stratification but also the unequal distribution of cultural knowledge and formal education, with habitus revealing this dynamic. His theory of cultural reproduction connects economic position, social status, and symbolic capital with cultural knowledge and skills, demonstrating how the unequal distribution of economic, cultural, and symbolic resources is at stake in social competition among individuals. Social competition is always a struggle, not only for and between economic capital but also for and among all forms of capital. The key forms of capital, that is, the resources that individuals draw on to gain advantage in society, are as follows:

- *Economic capital*: wealth, income, and other economic resources individuals can rely on.
- *Cultural capital*: the accumulated stock of knowledge gained within the family environment and through formal education. It is multidimensional, consisting of:
  - Embodied capital: informally gained through socialization and internalized in the form of habitus.

- Objectified capital: cultural objects that carry symbolic or traditional value.
- Institutionalized capital: formal knowledge typically leading to qualifications, degrees, diplomas, and other credentials.
- *Social capital*: involvement in reliable social networks that create mutual boundaries and mutual advantage. It emphasizes the importance of social connections over individual knowledge or skills, facilitating access to privileged positions and elite circles.
- *Symbolic capital*: the "aura" of prestige, status, and other forms of honor that surround individuals with high social standing. Symbolic capital operates within the communicative space, influencing how others perceive and confer honor upon individuals.

It is clear that capital is not simply a matter of possessed assets but of exchangeable assets. Therefore, they are not fixed endowments but rather likely to become capitals as long as they are relevant and can be exchanged with each other. The characteristic of this dynamic concept of capital is that they can be converted into one another, for example, social capital into economic capital or economic capital into symbolic capital, compensating for the lack of some capital with other forms of capital. The transformability of one form of capital into another is determined by its relevance in the field where the exchange takes place. Relevance in the field acts as a barrier to the interchangeability of capitals and helps to trace and maintain boundaries between different areas, which are often social and class-based.

Broadly speaking, Bourdieu's framework remains valid and widely used today to capture the dynamics behind the celebrification of certain culinary styles, especially among elites. It centers on a theoretical triad (Dobbin, 2008), which integrates socially shaped individual agency (habitus) with the power relations at play at a given moment (competition for economic, cultural, and social capital) within a given socially organized structure (the field). This model can be applied to many fields of human consumption, but especially to gastronomy, where the association between food and an individual's standing is a long-established concept, epitomized by Brillat-Savarin's claim, "Tell me what you eat, and I will tell you who you are" (1986 [1825], p. 3).

Gastronomic knowledge or certain incorporated knowledge that is pertinent to one field (e.g., catering, running a restaurant) may not be relevant to another (e.g., academic pathways in gastronomic sciences, food technology, food journalism, or scientific dissemination). Being a good cook or a renowned chef is not sufficient to become a tenured professor of culinary arts or food sociology, nor is it enough to become a gastronomic journalist. Similarly, being a journalist does not qualify one to be a professor, and being a professor, cook, or journalist does not necessarily qualify one to be a successful entrepreneur or CEO in the food industry. The assets (money, culture, relationships, and reputation) acquired within one sector must be recognized as valid and useful according to the rules of the field in which they are to be exchanged in order to gain a position within that field. The more pillars and rules a field has, the more difficult it will be to gain access to it. However, symbolic capital, as a reputational enhancer, has the peculiarity of being a resource in itself, functioning like a currency that confers credibility and facilitates the exchange between other forms of capital. However, symbolic capital, as a reputational enhancer, has the peculiarity of being a resource in itself, functioning like a currency that confers credibility and facilitates the exchange between other forms of capital. To fulfill this function, symbolic capital, operated by media, often works in combination with social capital, where social ties become the channels for disseminating reputation. In the field of gastronomy, traditional media such as gastronomic guides, cookbooks, and television cooking shows, alongside various forms of social media over the past two decades – including recipe websites, serious/leisure gastronomic journalism, and food blogs, but also travel social media such as Instagram, Facebook, and TikTok – have captured this dynamic in depth and implemented it in their user engagement strategies. With the policy of likes and rewards, transforming ratings into rankings and enabling earnings based on followers, social media monetizes the popularity gained through intensive use of their platforms by figures from the culinary professions, such as chefs. The extensive and pervasive dissemination capacity of both traditional media and social media enhances the popularity of these figures, transforming it into influence and granting them access to fields that were previously inaccessible, such as obtaining a university professorship. By increasing social capital, (social) media enriches that initial cultural capital – the chef's expertise relevant only in the specific field of cooking – into economic capital (earnings from the number of followers). This popularity is capitalized in symbolic terms, becoming influence (symbolic capital), transforming that practical expertise into reputation and credibility – in a word, status – opening the doors to academic teaching, scientific dissemination, and journalism (cultural capital).

Of course, there are cases where the popularity already existed, and social media simply amplified it at every level. It's the case of Ferran Adrià, a Spanish chef who invented molecular gastronomy and is considered one of the greatest chefs in the world. He teaches courses on "culinary physics" at the prestigious Harvard School of Engineering and Applied Sciences in Cambridge, Massachusetts. It's also the case of the great Italian chef Gualtiero Marchesi (who passed away a few years ago), who served as the Rector of the Alma International School of Italian Cuisine. Another example is Fulvio Pierangelini, Italy's top chef for many years, who was a lecturer in "Aesthetics and Gastronomic Creation" at the Physics Faculty of the University of Parma and at the University of Gastronomic Sciences in Pollenzo, a pioneering university in food studies. And then there's Massimo Bottura, owner of the highly acclaimed Osteria Francescana in Modena, who has taught at Alma and Pollenzo, and gives lectures at prestigious Italian universities like Bocconi University in Milan and the University of Bologna on design and creativity in cuisine.[8]

3.6 "Taste classifies, and it classifies the classifier": Taste still marking social borders in the contemporary society

In contrast to a tradition that dates back to time immemorial, which has always considered taste as an indisputable idiosyncratic attitude ("de gustibus non est disputandum"), and thus as an exclusive expression of subjectivity that escapes judgment, Bourdieu's perspective is revolutionary, as it categorizes taste among the highly debatable aesthetic forms of judgment, considering it an expression of social stratification and, even, of its legitimization and reproduction. "Taste classifies, and it classifies the classifier": With this famous statement, Bourdieu (1984, p. 6) expressed the socially shaped nature of taste and its active role in drawing class-based distinctions between individuals, which forms the core of

---

[8] *Ferran Adrià sarà docente ad Harvard e in Italia sempre più chef negli atenei - Corriere Roma.* (n.d.). https://roma.corriere.it/notizie/cronaca/10_marzo_25/ adria-chef-prof-harvard-1602716087126.shtml.

his distinction theory. Even today, forty years later, taste – which in the meantime has become the altar to which the food market is devoted as the highest symbol of individual and personal expression through food choices – continues to play a significant role in defining social boundaries in contemporary society. It distinguishes not only between categories of luxury, freedom, and necessity but also delineates individuals' social status.

Social subjects, who are classified by their classifications, are in turn distinguished – and classified – by the distinctions they make between the beautiful and the ugly, the genteel and the vulgar, wherein their position in the objective classifications is expressed or betrayed. Food-related choices are particularly influenced by this theory because, in addition to the many dimensions of taste, they involve the ideal of the body shaped by an individual's habitus, which, as argued before, is not individually determined.

> Tastes in food also depend on the idea each class has of the body and of the effects of food on the body, that is, on its strength, health, and beauty [...] it follows that the body is the most indisputable materialization of class taste. (Bourdieu, 1984, p. 190)

If we consider the social space, as Bourdieu did, as an arena primarily defined by two forms of endowments that individuals possess as members of class fractions – economic capital and cultural capital – we can recognize in their tastes, lifestyles, and consumer preferences aspirational strategies of competition. These strategies aim to gain or prove the status of the immediately higher class fraction they aspire to resemble while distancing themselves from the immediately lower class fraction they do not want to be associated with. Following Bourdieu, we can specifically focus on the food-related dimension of these tastes and propensions so as to have a four-quadrant chart, akin to Bourdieu's food-space (Bourdieu, 1984, p. 186), where individuals position themselves based on their educational background, incomes, and specific occupational status to form clusters exhibiting corresponding tastes (Figure 3).

The upper classes are characterized by their wealth in both economic and cultural capital, enabling them to afford the best choices, and they are often positioned in the upper-right quadrant of the chart. Their appearance authentically reflects their substantial wealth without needing to disguise their status. Tastemakers, who belong to these groups, wield influence by shaping the tastes of others through their abundant economic and cultural resources. They establish norms and embody what is often termed "legitimate taste," commonly referred to simply as "taste" or "classical."

The upper-middle classes, enriched by both economic and cultural backgrounds, are distinguished by a "taste of freedom," indicating their ability to make choices in food consumption without significant economic constraints, alongside a refined sense of discernment. On their tables, you can find a range of offerings, from rare and expensive luxury foods to the finest cuts of meat and fish, as well as lighter, healthier, and innovative food options.

This taste places increasing emphasis on slimness, refined yet healthy eating habits, and becomes increasingly critical of coarseness and excess weight. Their emphasis on slimness and moderation evokes a sense of discipline and self-control as part of a civilizing process, as theorized by Elias (1983 [1969]), marking a triumph of culture over natural bodily appetites.

> The members of the professions are mainly distinguished by the high proportion of their spending which goes on expensive products, particularly meat (18.3 percent of their food budget), and especially the most expensive meat (veal, lamb, mutton), fresh fruit and vegetables, fish and shellfish, cheese and aperitifs [...] the taste of the professionals or senior executives defines the popular taste, by negation, as the taste for the heavy, the fat and the coarse, by tending towards the light, the refined and the delicate [...]. The disappearance of economic constraints is accompanied by a strengthening of the social censorships which forbid coarseness and fatness, in favour of slimness and distinction. The taste for rare, aristocratic foods points to a traditional cuisine, rich in expensive or rare products (fresh vegetables, meat). (Bourdieu, 1984, p. 185)

Class fractions characterized by newly acquired high economic capital but low or absent cultural capital, such as industrial and commercial employers, craftsmen, and small shopkeepers, are often referred to as the *nouveaux riches*, and they might occupy the lower-right quadrant of the food space. These individuals have recently experienced economic affluence, which enables them to ease economic constraints. However, their lack of cultural capital, often evidenced by lower levels of education and refined tastes, means their preferences for strong or fatty foods, or large portions, may not fundamentally change. The *nouveaux riches* are those individuals or groups who have recently acquired wealth but lack institutionalized cultural capital in their background, resulting in less refined habitus and sometimes being perceived as vulgarly ostentatious or lacking in social graces. They often engage in conspicuous consumption and display their wealth materially without fully adopting the cultural norms and tastes of the traditional upper classes.

They may attempt to emulate the upper classes by consuming expensive foods or using dining experiences to enhance their social status (such as aperitifs or dining occasions to mingle with higher echelons). As a result, they frequent prestigious and selective establishments such as three-star Michelin restaurants or luxury hotels. However, their preference for quantity, stemming from their origins, persists in their habitus. This tendency leads them to consume increasingly lavish and calorie-rich foods, transforming the act of eating (la *bouffe*) into a grand feast (la *grande bouffe*) (Bourdieu, 1984, p. 185).

> Thus, when one moves from the manual workers to the industrial and commercial employers, through foremen, craftsmen and small shopkeepers, economic constraints tend to relax without any fundamental change in the pattern of spending [...]. The opposition between the two extremes is here established between the poor and the rich (nouveau riche), between la *bouffe* and la *grande bouffe*; the food consumed is increasingly rich (both in cost and in calories) and increasingly heavy (game, foie gras). [...] (Bourdieu, 1984, p. 185)

The social groups occupying the area tending toward the cross-point of the food chart, between the "lower" fractions of the upper class (high cultural capital and good to average economic capital), the "higher" fractions of the *nouveaux riches* (high economic capital but average to low cultural capital), and, albeit to a limited extent, the higher fractions of the lower classes (average cultural capital and middle to low economic capital), are those more committed to symbolic competition, as they are engaged in social climbing. These middle-class groups, like teachers, white collars, rich in "cultural capital," if not economic capital, are particularly committed to the symbolic value of their choices, since they *tend to emphasize interest in novelty*, as *a sign of their cultural capital that becomes the main resource they draw on in their aspiration to copy the choices and behaviors of the upper classes*; cultural background gains a symbolic value as long as it works as a surrogate for their limited economic resources. They tend to maintain their distinctiveness by cultivating tastes for exotic and foreign foods, characteristics that allude to a curious mindset that leans on broad stocks of accumulated knowledge (cultural capital). The phenomenon of dining out and the choice of restaurants where this kind of food are served is particularly demonstrative of this. Moreover, the middle classes routinely avoid being seen in low-class eateries, typically characterized by the presence of junk food, while they are open to "popular food" or "traditional food" as a sign of open-mindedness, appreciation of traditional cuisines as forms of intangible heritage.

> Finally, the teachers, richer in cultural capital than in economic capital, and therefore inclined to ascetic consumption in all areas, pursue originality at the lowest economic cost and go in for exoticism (Italian, Chinese cooking etc) and culinary populism (peasant dishes). They are thus almost consciously opposed to the (new) rich with their rich food, the buyers and sellers of *grosse bouffe*, the "fat cats," gross in body and mind, who have the economic means to flaunt, with an arrogance perceived as 'vulgar', a life-style which remains very close to that of the working classes as regards economic and cultural consumption. (Bourdieu, 1984, p. 185)

Middle-class tastes often demonstrate a preference for frozen food, which serves as a convenient compromise. This choice is particularly suitable for middle-class women who typically work outside the home and have limited time for cooking. Indeed, Bourdieu considers eating habits – especially when represented solely by the produce consumed – as inseparable from the whole lifestyle of the individuals involved, and lifestyles are strongly influenced by gender roles and the division of workload inside and outside the household. In addition to economic and cultural backgrounds, time and gender become important factors in defining lifestyles, eating styles, and consumer preferences, thereby distinguishing tastes. Frozen food offers a practical solution that aligns with their desire for convenience while also meeting their preference for healthy and nutritious options.

> The most obvious reason for this is that the taste for particular dishes (of which the statistical shopping-basket gives only the vaguest idea) is associated, through preparation and cooking, with a whole conception of the do-

mestic economy and of the division of labour between the sexes. A taste for elaborate casserole dishes (pot-au-feu, blanquette, daube), which demand a big investment of time and interest, is linked to a traditional conception of woman's role. Thus, there is a particularly strong opposition in this respect between the working classes and the dominated fractions of the dominant class, in which the women, whose labour has a high market value (and who, perhaps as a result, have a higher sense of their own value) tend to devote their spare time rather to child care and the transmission of cultural capital, and to contest the traditional division of domestic labour. The aim of saving time and labour in preparation combines with the search for light, low-calorie products, and points towards grilled meat and fish, raw vegetables ('salades composees'), frozen foods, yogurt and other milk products, all of which are diametrically opposed to popular dishes, the most typical of which is pot-au-feu, made with cheap meat that is boiled (as opposed to grilled or roasted), a method of cooking that chiefly demands time. It is no accident that this form of cooking symbolizes one state of female existence and of the sexual division of labour (a woman entirely devoted to housework is called 'pot-au-feu'), just as the slippers put on before dinner symbolize the complementary male role. (Bourdieu, 1984, pp. 188–189)

Research (Øygard, 2000) proves that still today, groups rich in cultural capital are more interested in healthy and exotic food and less in filling food than those possessing less cultural capital, marking the line between well-educated consumers and *nouveaux riches*, as well as between the taste of freedom and the taste of necessity. The bourgeoisie is therefore disingenuous in the way they adopt or shape cultural tastes to differentiate themselves from the lower classes and to gain some semblance of the upper ones, nevertheless ever conscious of their real rank within society, and never at ease with being such as they are (hence their pretentious semblance and the paradoxical awkward effect in their effort to appear "natural"). *Bourdieu betrays a subtle contempt for the middle classes' pretentiousness and lack of authenticity. The middle class struggles to appear as they "pretend to be," and behave in such a way as to appear as close as possible to the social ideal to which they aspire.*

The lower classes, lacking both economic and cultural capital and constrained by economic limitations, often find themselves excluded from both real and symbolic competitions. Their tastes are genuine expressions of their circumstances. According to Bourdieu, the working class and peasants exhibit a "taste for necessity," which emphasizes the most filling and economical foods as a means of alleviating economic constraints through food consumption (Bourdieu, 1984, p. 6).

This taste involves allocating a significant portion of their income to food, sometimes to the point where it becomes an unavoidable ration due to their very low incomes. Preferences in the taste for necessity prioritize practicality and substance: they favor larger quantities of bread for immediate energy, fat-rich foods such as pork, milk, and cheese for sustenance, and larger portions overall as a measure of substance. These choices are driven not by a desire for social status or appearance but by economic necessity. As a result, their tastes are sincere, unaffected, and focused on substance rather than appearance or cultural norms associated with higher classes. This distinction underscores how food preferences can reflect and respond to the economic realities and social positions of different class groups. However, what the lower classes perceive as unpretentious, straightforward, and comforting due to its familiarity, may be viewed by the middle and upper classes as lacking refinement and propriety. This disparity highlights the distinct cultural perceptions and values associated with food and consumption across social classes.

> Substance – or matter – is what is substantial, not only 'filling' but also real, as opposed to all appearances, all the fine words and empty gestures that 'butter no parsnips' and are, as the phrase goes, purely symbolic; reality, as against sham, imitation, window-dressing [...]
> It is the free-speech and language of the heart which make the true 'nice guy', blunt, straightforward, unbending, honest, genuine, 'straight down the line' and 'straight as a die', as opposed to everything that is pure form, done only for form's sake; it is freedom and the refusal of complications, as opposed to respect for all the forms and formalities spontaneously perceived as instruments of distinction and power. On these moralities, these world views, there is no neutral viewpoint; what for some is shameless and slovenly, for others is straightforward, unpretentious; familiarity is for some the most absolute form of recognition, the abdication of all distance, a trusting openness, a relation of equal to equal; for others, who shun familiarity, it is an unseemly liberty (Bourdieu, 1984, p. 199).

3.7   Rethinking Bourdieu's food chart in the current food space

Trying to update the famous graph representing the lifestyles and food tastes of the different class fractions that Bourdieu (1984, p. 187) drew up in late 1970s France, we could imagine a scenario like the one depicted in Figure 3.

As argued before, most of the symbolic competition for taste distinction involves middle-class groups endowed with middle-to-low or middle-to-high cultural and economic capital. Their food choices represent their attempt to exchange their resources for the capitals they lack, in order to appropriate as much as possible the legitimate taste of the tastemakers, who occupy the upper-right quadrant, rich in both economic and cultural capital.

The underlying distinctive dynamic appears to be confirmed: the taste of freedom and that of necessity serve as the great dividing lines between rich and poor social groups. The strategic use of culture, curiosity, and discernment marks the taste and consumption choices of the middle classes with medium-high cultural capital (the *connoisseurs*), though they may not be very affluent economically (upper-left quadrant of the food chart). The *nouveaux riches* (lower-right quadrant) strategically use their recent economic availability by directing their increased spending capacity toward ostentatious consumption typically linked to social occasions, attempting to mask their lack of education and still seeking legitimacy in the echelons of the elites. However, despite everything, they still retain the patterns of the taste of necessity, oriented toward quantity rather than quality and conviviality (the Bouffe becomes Grand). These two groups, diametrically opposed and characterized by their mutual negation, also distinguish themselves through opposing forms of taste: the *connoisseurs* exhibit an aware, curious, and critical taste, with a preference for convenience and thrifty choices. They are also more open to introducing new elements into their diet or switching to new, healthy, and sustainable diets compatible with their economic standing. The *nouveaux riches* exhibit a taste for conspicuous and extravagant choices to emulate tastemakers. However, unlike them, their consumption is uncritical and conformist, still influenced by the indulgence of the taste of necessity from their origins, which they seek to hide and disguise as abundance.

Figure 3   An heuristically updated chart of Bourdieu's food chart[9]

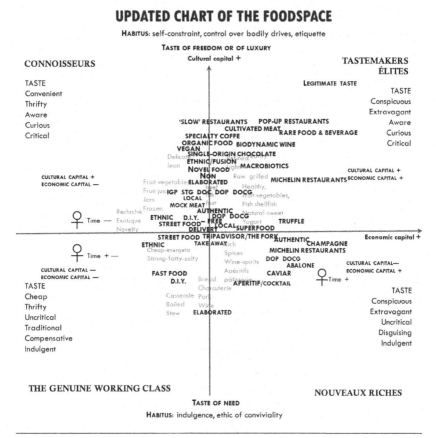

UPDATED CHART OF THE FOODSPACE

Source: Author's revisitation of Bourdieu's chart of food space from his seminal work *Distinction* (1984, p. 187), adapted to the current foodscape.

The *tastemakers*, richest in all forms of capital, though still inclined toward conspicuously appropriating rare foods and the extravagance such rarity implies, in times of ecological transition and resource crisis, tend to

---

[9] The chart's depiction of tastes for various foods is based on heuristically attributed tastes related to socio-economic standings rather than statistical measurements. These attributions are derived from over 240 interviews with students attending the Graduate Degree in "Food Innovation and Management" at the University of Gastronomic Sciences, which aimed to apply Bourdieu's theory to the current foodscape.

move away from traditional wasteful styles and behave more like responsible consumers. They partly embrace innovation to support sustainability while also returning to the simplicity of natural eating habits. Confirming the trickle-down model discussed above, they begin adopting the natural, "slow," and simple eating patterns traditionally associated with rural lower classes to showcase their conscientious and responsible approach to food consumption amid scarcity.

This adaptation represents a form of responsibilization but also entails the aesthetic colonization of eating patterns by lower classes. Once these patterns become fashionable among affluent groups, they become less accessible to the lower classes. The members of the working classes and of dominated ethnic groups, whom Bourdieu identified as genuine "poors," "with their cult for cleanness and honesty" as a point of honor "to belie the image that the dominant have of their class" (1984, p. 588), are largely excluded from this symbolic competition, often relegated to unhealthy and uncritical consumption due to affordability constraints. Nonetheless, their detachment from the dynamics of distinction allows them to maintain authenticity and serves as a form of resistance against superficial trends pursued solely for appearances' sake. The preference for "strong" food and drink in the eating patterns of both the peasant class and the industrial working class cannot be reduced to the need to fill up at the lowest cost. Though constrained by need, these social groups have a taste that often exalts strength and, at times, virility, characteristics related to the peculiar condition of these classes within the work chain. Being rich only in their labor power, they are expected to use the force of their bodies to carry out their heavy work and exercise (Bourdieu, 1984, p. 384). Their labor relies on the physical strength and courage of its members, and food should nourish this power they contribute to society.

Finally, the significant and enduring takeaway from Bourdieu's lesson, which is still reflected in the above food chart depicting the contemporary food space, is that the rich and the poor develop their habits and tastes by virtue of their concrete experiences and their functions in the social arena. In this sense, taste is a social construction.

3.8   The culinary skills as a form of capital at omnivorous times

Bourdieu's concept of cultural capital found fertile uses in later sociological studies of food consumers, particularly focusing on the importance of food-related knowledge in contemporary consumption dynamics. Peter Naccarato and Kathleen LeBesco (2012) coined the term "culinary capital," a concept deeply indebted to the French sociologist's idea that individuals acquire status and power by accessing multiple forms of capital. Following Bourdieu's example, they particularly emphasize how individuals' food-related practices, skills, and knowledge – especially their ability to articulate them (narration being the current mode of display) – are implicated in reputational dynamics and the acquisition of status. The way these practices are involved in the circulation and exchange of capitals, promoting individuals' social mobility, defines them as a distinct form of culinary capital. Like Bourdieu, Naccarato and LeBesco (2012) recognize that food and food practices play a unique role as markers of social status. They focus on the way in which different consumers use types of food to gain reputation, credibility as *connoisseurs* with a good experience of the world, and position themselves in fields of status. They start from Bourdieu's ideas to consider how a variety of cultural institutions, including marketing and advertising, cable television, internet communities, festival celebrations, and spectacular contexts function to socialize individuals. More broadly, they read individuals' use of their food practices as a way to create and sustain identities that align with their society's norms and expectations and, in some cases, as proper efforts to participate in projects of citizenship; these can be read as attempts to acquire culinary capital.

In the same vein of valuing strategic uses of culinary knowledge as a form of capital in late-modern, culturally omnivorous societies, Warren Belasco highlighted the link between dietary choices and both individual and group identity formation. He also anticipated the political, particularly countercultural uses of food to resist mainstream cultural logics in American way of life of early Nineties, and to pioneer new paradigms of consumption and production (Belasco, 2005). At the beginning of the so called "cultural turn" in consumption, culinary knowledge emerged as a significant language to promote countercuisine, serving as a practice to legitimize countercultural tastes:

> By categorizing foods into what's good to eat and what is not, a cuisine helps a society's members define themselves. To eat appropriate foods is to participate in a particular group; to eat inappropriate food means that you are an outsider. Like language, a cuisine is a medium by which a society establishes its special identity. (Belasco, 1989, p. 44)

This is one of the reasons why, in global societies characterized by omnivorous culture, the seek for "authenticity" has become the new pattern
for social distinction (Oleschuk, 2016). And this is one of the reasons
why "authenticity" is trending in virtual communities. Moreover, culinary capital plays an important role in the "investment of power in the
body" (Foucault, 1980, 56), as it both promotes normative standards of
the "healthy" body and authorizes indulgences and excesses that oppose
such cultural expectations. The tension between health (self-control) and
indulgence (self-satisfying) conjures up the paradox of the principle of incorporation (the body as a demarcation line between inside and outside).

3.9   From taste standardization to taste differentiation: The cultural turn in late-modern consumption

Taste standardization, especially in the realm of food, epitomizes the
postwar expansion of capitalist commodity production, giving rise to
a vast accumulation of consumer goods. After the Second World War,
economic recovery, primarily led by the United States, shifted many
capitalist economies' focus from production and labor to consumption.
Profit generation transitioned from the production-consumption relationship to the dynamics of credit and debt, as predicted by Max Weber.
Simultaneously, the economic center moved from industry and factories
to shopping centers. The consumer experience became paramount, leading shopping centers to evolve into large supermarkets and department
stores. These spaces fulfilled the dream of affordability, making them
accessible to countless purchasers.

This led to the rise of mass society, marked by the collapse of an informed and critically independent public into an unstructured, amor-
phous, and largely apathetic mass.

The prerogative of mass culture is an ever greater and more varied
offer, which seeks to satisfy not only the demand of the wealthy sections
of society but also the taste of all, that is, all tastes. Taste are standardized to average (e.g., mediocre), fleeting expectations are met, and goods
are produced in enormous quantities, whether literary products, music or
visual art, food, or cultural creations.

The economic model behind the mass production society is known as
"Fordism," that is, a macroeconomic regime of accumulation that sup-

ports expanded reproduction and whose growth is based on mass production and mass consumption. Fordist "mass production" is typically based on a technical division of labor organized along assembly line techniques that exploit the semi-skilled labor of the "mass worker"; other types of workers (artisans or unskilled workers, foremen, engineers, designers, etc.) are also employed, but elsewhere. Another typical feature of Fordism is the systematic control of all stages of accumulation, from raw material production to commercialization by one and the same company (see Siegel and Vale, 1988, p. 5). Fordism has been associated with continuing commodification, bureaucratization, social homogenization, and individualization, and this is reflected not only in economic and political life but also in the cultural sphere (Jessop, 1992). As highlighted by Harvey (1989):

> Postwar Fordism has to be seen, therefore, less as a mere system of mass production and more as a total way of life. Mass production meant standardization of product as well as mass consumption; and that meant a whole new aesthetic and a commodification of culture. (Harvey 1989, p. 135)

The paradigm of Fordist mass consumption in late modern society and its further post-Fordist development were paradigmatically described with the term "McDonaldization." This term was coined by the American sociologist George Ritzer (1998), who identified this standardization of taste in the logic of fast food restaurants. They are geared toward extreme standardization of their offerings and maximizing profits by reaching the largest possible number of consumers.

In Ritzer's words:

> McDonaldization is the major example of, and the paradigm for, a wide-ranging process by which the principles of the fast-food restaurant are coming to dominate more and more sectors of American society as well as of the rest of the world (Ritzer, 1998). The focus of McDonaldization is consumption, which has come to rival, even exceed, the importance of production, especially in high developed nations like the United States. It is this that leads to the conclusion that the fast-food restaurant, whose home is obviously in the realm of consumption, is a better paradigm today for rationalization or McDonaldization of society. (Ritzer, 1998)

McDonaldization relies on four primary dimensions: Efficiency, calcu-
lability, predictability, and control, whose resulting effect is nevertheless
often one of irrationality. In other words, as we try to become efficient
(e.g., every aspect of the organization is geared toward the minimiza-
tion of time), calculable (e.g., quantity takes over quality), predictable
(e.g., standardized and uniform services, so that a person can walk into
any McDonald's in the world and receive the same sandwiches prepared
in the same way), and controlling (standardized and uniform employ-
ees, easily replaceable by nonhuman technologies), we often end up with
illogical, counterintuitive, and problematic results. Exactly the consequences brought about by mass consumption, whose relentless logic of
the commodity led to an oversupply of symbolic goods and the inflation up to saturation of values attached to objects. Anyway, this business
model of food supply and consumption has proven to be very flexible
and able to keep up with the most important social changes of our times
and their consequences on consumer trends: The rise of postindustrial,
post-Fordist, and postmodern society.

3.9.1 *The rise of postmodern society: The recoup of individuality over the mass. "Diminishing contrasts and increasing varieties"*

The main feature of a postindustrial economy is a phase of growth within
an industrialized economy or nation in which the relative importance of
the manufacturing industry decreases and the importance of services,
information, and research increases. A post-Fordist economy is one in
which the prevailing production processes, strategies and paradigms are
characterized by a high degree of product innovation, a flexible production process based on flexible machinery or systems, a correspondingly
flexible workforce (flexibility in terms of the level of functions and skills,
the duration and form of the employment contract, the wage package,
etc.), and worker responsibility (a flexible workforce) and worker responsibility (a shift from the primacy of the hierarchical, well-resourced, bu-
reaucratic "Sloan" form of corporate structure to flatter, leaner and more
flexible forms of organization). Another feature of the Fordist period is
the increasing emphasis on differentiated forms of consumption, with
commercial capital being reorganized to create and serve increasingly segmented markets. The hypermarket, the shopping center, and the
boutique are often cited as archetypal post-Fordist forms of consumption

and contrasted with the supermarkets and department stores typical of Fordist mass consumption (Jessop, 1992). A postmodern society is characterized by the culmination of a process in which constant change has become the status quo, even at an individual level, and the notion of progress has become obsolete. In a postmodern world, truth and reality are understood to be individually shaped by personal history, social class, gender, culture, and religion, but above all by personal experience, with no universal or predetermined application of truth. Postmodernism emphasizes differences, plurality, and selective forms of tolerance.

A sharp critique of the oversaturation with myriad cultural associations and illusions conveyed by commodities can be found in the work of Jean Baudrillard (1988). He notes the obliterating effect on reality created by the manipulative use of signs in media and advertising: "Commodity signs," mere signifiers detached from concrete objects, are available for a variety of associative relationships, effectively killing the real world and giving rise to a new order of meanings.

The "seductive" promise of consumer goods to fulfill dreams, fueled by personalized desires and proliferating sites of consumption, often overshadows other factors associated with consumption. An "attack on the unconscious" (Vance Packard) had already been launched long before by hidden persuaders – the advertisers – who inundate consumers with images of romance, exoticism, longing, beauty, fulfillment, community, innovation, and mundane meanings associated with consumer goods like soap, washing machines, cars, alcoholic beverages, and more. Their aim is to emotionally engage consumers in a generalized, comfortable ideal of life.

> We no longer buy oranges, we buy vitality. We do not buy just an auto, we buy prestige. (Packard, 1957, p. 8)

Marketers are increasingly emphasizing sensory overload, aesthetic immersion, and dreamlike perceptions of decentralized subjects, where individuals open themselves to a wider range of sensations and emotional experiences. This trend sets the conditions for the transition from mass society to what is termed "postmodern" society.

In mass society, although pluralistic, coherence prevailed. The mass consumer remained predictable and controllable, driven by the collective need for identification satisfied through consumption amid the vast standardization of tastes. Postmodern society, however, witnesses a rise in the desire for differentiation, leading to the fragmentation of consumer identities and the emergence of diverse social bonds – a phenomenon Maffesoli terms "tribalism." The pursuit of the "logo" symbolizes the widespread demand for personalized consumption and the narrowing of identity to immediate, individualistic experiences. Traditional temples of consumption like department stores and supermarkets are evolving into "malls" – vast, roofed shopping spaces resembling boulevards and urban hubs. Here, consumption transforms into a holistic experience, departing from mere transactional encounters to embody the dream of "affordable leisure" once exclusive to the elite, now accessible as a personal and distinctive exploration within these artificial cities.

Postmodern society is marked by the so-called "cultural turn," a new wave started in the 1980s until the turn of the twenty-first century, *where consumer attention shifts from the instrumental aspects of consumption to its symbolic dimensions, and especially to consumer goods' capacity for communicating personal meaning.*

The cultural turn has been understood by many scholars as a consequence of the decline of social class and economic constraints on individual action, and the increasing need for individuals' cultural differentiation in their strategies of identity definition. As a matter of fact, an implication of such a cultural turn is the capacity for commodities to break down social barriers, to dissolve the long-established links between persons and things. The countertendency, however, is a movement toward de-commodification and to restrict, control, and channel the exchange of goods.

The growing prominence of the *culture* of consumption also means that consumption can no longer be regarded as derived unproblematically from production, and consumer needs for differentiation are no longer simply derived from the social contrasts created by the contradictions of the class system. Stephen Mennell synthesizes such a trend in the formula "Diminishing contrasts, increasing varieties" (1985, p. 319). He emphasizes the cultural and symbolic value of consumption, especially in the field of food consumption, to support the thesis of a decline of class determinism in taste and the advance of an alternative, pluralist thesis.

Overall, the trend is towards more people in England and France having the opportunity for more varied experience in eating and to develop more varied tastes [...] underneath the many swirling cross currents, the main trend has been towards diminishing contrasts and increasing varieties in food habits and culinary taste. One trend, not two: for in spite of the apparent contradiction between diminishing contrasts and increasing varieties, these are both facets of the same processes. (Mennell, 1985, pp. 321–22)

Indeed, Mennell sets this statement within a broader historical understanding of the evolution of mass society:

We have all along treated the way a society eats as an important part of its culture, so let us now examine the possibility of interpreting modern trends in cooking and eating in the light of theories of "mass culture." (Mennell, 1985, pp. 321–322)

According to his reading, for Western societies, mass production and consumption also meant a great increase in supply security. The general availability of food has been expanded, this brought about a reduction of social inequalities and an increase in the need for people to differentiate themselves within a huge availability of food supplies and thereby, attach cultural value to their food choices.

Process of (functional, not necessarily political) democratization during the past two centuries have ensured a more equal distribution of the accessibility of food to the population by the mechanism of wages (which went up) and prices which went down. (Mennell et al., 1992, p. 62)

The potential of consumer culture means going beyond the mere acquisition of goods, which is about how goods and services are obtained through different kinds of social and economic exchanges; it emphasizes "appropriation," which is what people do with goods once they acquire (purchase) them, and "appreciation," how things gain and lose value while appropriating them. Consumer "sovereignty" in postmodern consumeristic culture is largely based on the capability to alternate between these two dimensions, a strategic ability to move in and out of self-control so as to experience a wider range of sensations and enhance the propensity to consume.

If it is true that the everyday use of a tool, even if it is habituated to the extent that it has become more or less automatic (e.g., the using of a fork when eating a meal), still requires a symbolic meaning, the "culturalist" way of understanding consumption emphasizes, even to the point of exaggerating the individual's cognition and mental deliberation lying beyond food consumption. This makes eating a "purely" cultural, symbolic act, thus losing sight of its intrinsically material (Reckwitz, 2002), even routine nature. As a matter of fact, nowadays, food quality is determined less by abundant quantity and global provenance and more by sourcing (the more local, the better), artisanality (the smaller the run, the better), taste (the more organic, the better), sustainability, healthiness, and mindfulness of what is eaten. Probably, the attention to sustainability, responsibility, and ethicality – as new values that underpin our consumer choices, also advocated by SDG12 of the United Nations 2030 Agenda – suggests that a gastronomic capital is taking over the concept of "culinary" capital, which was once only concerned with cooking and eating. A person who has knowledge about wine and who can compare and contrast menus at high-end restaurants is regarded as a person with "culinary capital" – someone who has made a different, valuable investment in themselves and is therefore also rewarded with status and power. More broadly, even when individuals assert the value of certain dietary preferences and food practices over others, they are engaging themselves in the quest for culinary capital. However, a person who is able to discern the difference between local, clean, and sustainable foods, or to explain why eating locally produced food is recommendable but not enough to ensure a more sustainable food system – in general, someone who can connect the practices of cooking and eating to the broader edible space, encompassing the multiple and interconnected choices that human groups make in their natural environments to select, obtain, preserve, and only afterwards cook and eat food (Poulaine, 2017) – is not simply a person with culinary capital, but a person with gastronomic capital. This is an unprecedented form of cultural capital that will help consumers contribute to a better world.

3.10 "Neo-tribalism" in food consumption: The empathetic connection and the online communities as drivers of emerging food-related eating styles

If postmodernity designates the affirmation of the subject over the mass and emphasizes difference, plurality, and selective forms of tolerance, according to Maffesoli, postmodern forms of consumption represent a new aesthetic that transcends mere individualism. In previous theories addressing food-related dynamics, consumers have typically been viewed as individual actors. Although certain approaches, such as Bourdieu's and Warde's practice-theoretical framing of taste, have highlighted the relational and context-bound dynamics of taste formation and expression, consumers have always been portrayed as singular subjects engaged in their relationship with food. We must await Maffesoli's theorization of new patterns of sociality distinguishing late-modern societies to move beyond individualistic accounts of consumption, a dimension that even STS (Science and Technology Studies) frameworks of sociological analysis of human/digital interaction have not completely overcome.

> Between the 18th and the 20th centuries, modernity was built on rationalism, individualism (the individual seen as a unit) and on the social contract of the Republic, united and indivisible. The modernist project was to dominate nature and to be universal. The postmodernity which has succeeded it has seen the powerful return of the impulse to community and of the need of collective emotion – I call this neo-tribalism (1988). The plural person, identifying with a number of tribes and elective affinities based on common tastes, is rediscovering the importance of territory (roots) and 'compagnonnage' – the passing on of a trade and a craftsman's identity, an initiation rather than an education. It is this nascent postmodernity which I attempt to describe. (Maffesoli, 2016, p. 739)

According to Maffesoli's sociological account, new forms of identity seem to emerge, leaning on the blurring of the boundaries between individuals and groups and the emergence of a new, postmodern sociality, that replaces modern society and its sharp contrasts and needs for social classification. The move away from individualism and from its ideal of society built upon the rational individual seems to feature postmodernity, with its aesthetic paradigm relying on communal feelings and the search for temporary/transitive and emotional/affective communities. Maffesoli emphasizes affectivity and empathy as leverages for the rise of new consumer tastes and inclinations, whose proliferation is the basis for such a new aesthetic paradigm, in which masses of people tend to temporarily aggregate in fluid "postmodern tribes" (Maffesoli, 1996 [1988]). Maffesoli anticipates the current dynamics of lifestyle, in particular the online mechanisms for creating communities on platforms and social media, which have left behind the individualistic ideal of solitary consumption as described by Giddens (1991) in favor of a sense of community and the search for a new embeddedness facilitated by the community-building dynamics of digital communication.

Neo-tribes are *"groupes immediats"* and *"petites collectivities"* – temporary groupings and small collectives – which arise spontaneously before a more rational level of organization takes place. Territory is expressed by a reworked *myth of locality*, and the new "everybody" is the familiar, everyday, known world, "in other words, it is a tribal world" (Maffesoli, 2016, p. 743).

The three great characteristics of the tribal phenomenon are: the importance of the territory in which the tribe finds itself; the sharing of common tastes; and the return of the eternal child. All three are paradigmatic of the feeling of belonging, which is both the cause and effect of tribalism.

The paradigm of the "neo-tribe" draws inspiration from Durkheim's concepts of "ritual" and mechanical solidarity in a premodern world (Durkheim, 1984; Shilling and Mellor, 1998) and epitomizes the social potential of emotional bonds within cohesive, overlapping communities, being emblematic of postmodern sociality and identity formation. Despite emerging concerns about potential offense from the term "tribe," the paradigm does not portray this social configuration negatively, nor does it evoke false notions of obsessive conformity or irrational feelings associated with archaic tribalism. Instead, by celebrating the resurgence of communal bonds and affirming individual qualities through empathetic, albeit temporary, cohabitation (Maffesoli, 2016, pp. 743–744), this theory provides an epistemological account for current forms of ontological nomadism (Maffesoli, 1997) fostered by virtual environments and the opportunity they provide to experiment with multiple identities – an opportunity especially offered to minorities that can experience normative emancipation.

By the way, though the concept of the "neo-tribe" was coined before the advent of social media, the success of the neo-tribal paradigm in contemporary society cannot be separated from the new modes of socialization introduced by technological developments in digital social networks and platform environments. These spaces cultivate tastes and lifestyles, especially through their promotion of interstitial, transitive, and temporary forms of aggregation.

Even though neotribal consumers are moved by a fragmented search for small interstitial utopias experienced in everyday life, and can make their purchase or provide their feedback to their consumer experience in total solitude from their rooms with their smartphones, their tastes are never totally disconnected. They are rather always stirred by the effort to heighten solitary choices into a collective emotion, and social media play a crucial role in underpinning such an affective tribalism. The fragmented self of the single user/consumer joining a blog in an app or a group in social media comes to be channeled into a larger self, the self of the tribe, mostly a meaning community whose socialization mainly takes place online, where everything is "relative" and what predominates is "an ever-shifting" sincerity, which is also an ever-shifting innocence. As Maffesoli himself states, these new communities of shared taste

> are no longer engaged in a search for a distant and abstract utopia with some kind of rational basis, but who are looking instead for a little utopia of a fragmentary nature which they can experience here there and everywhere and in the here and now. (Maffesoli, 2016, p. 746)

This paradigm has significantly influenced various academic fields by countering discourses of social fragmentation and individualization, particularly in consumer research. From Cova and Cova's emphasis on "connection through the object of consumption" (2002) to recent reappraisals of neotribal theory in leading food consumption studies (Hardy et al., 2018) and tourism (Vorobjovas-Pinta, 2021; Vorobjovas-Pinta and Lewis, 2021; Hardy et al., 2021), ongoing reflections address the need for emotionally based forms of social attachment and flexible social interaction, alongside the establishment of new symbolic boundaries, particularly within alternative food practices (le Grand, 2018) and vegetarian communities (Bertella, 2018).

Maffesoli's paradigm remains highly relevant and particularly suited to capture the types of connections that characterize online environments and the emerging socially embedded consumer dynamics on food platforms, especially the link between the emotional repertoire of restaurant reviews and the segmentation of dietary profiles within the community. Digital marketing capitalizes on this online social dynamic by appealing to consumers' desire for communal connectedness rather than mere consumption (Lupton and Feldman, 2020). Let's consider the use of "affordances," understood as "multi-layered, relational structures" that connect devices and users, enabling or constraining behavior in specific contexts (Evans et al., 2017). These affordances aim to enhance empathetic connections and consequently facilitate the release of emotional information about oneself.

In digital vegan communities promoting "caring" dietary styles, where health, ethics, and the environment are key motivators for sustainable food choices (Scott, 2020), affordances play a crucial role in building emotional connections around reviews and legitimizing valuable dietary choices that extend beyond the diet itself (Giraud, 2021). This phenomenon can be found in popular platforms of plant-based restaurant reviews, such as "HappyCow,"[10] where the rating of vegan restaurants and providing detailed information about offer, service, restaurant "ethos," environment, atmosphere, and price, contribute to the formation of a cocreated, non-preexisting knowledge, and the flux of empathetic and solidary communication imbues these reviews with ethical meanings, elevating them to identity markers (Greenebaum, 2012; Gummerus et al., 2015).

Here are some examples of plant-based restaurant reviews published on the platform "HappyCow." Reviewers on this platform are awarded distinctive labels based on their profile, visibility, and credibility within the community, which are determined by their active participation:

> Review of an Italian full vegan restaurant in Aosta Valley (Italy):
> Evaluation in Points: 5 stars
> Title: 'So healthy!'
> Review: Great place, so nice to have a healthy detox from pasta and pizza! Fridge full of trays of about 10 vegan foods to choose from. No pricing info before you get the bill, but it seems you can have a plate of 3 things, they'll heatup the ones that should be hot, and it's about 3-5 euros per item, so 12-15 a plate. Served on single use compostable plates & cutlery.
> Pro: everything delicious.
> Picture of the ordered plates.
>
> Review of an Italian full vegan restaurant in Aosta Valley (Italy):
> Evaluation in Points: 5 stars
> Title: 'Reimagined traditional dishes'
> Review: This vegan restaurant seamlessly blends delectable flavors with reimagined traditional dishes, elevating the dining experience. The owner's warm hospitality adds a delightful touch to the overall atmosphere.

---

[10] See: www.happycow.net (accessed on 16/07/2024).

Pro: 100% plant-based, Tasty dishes, Hospitality.
Contro: a bit expensive.
Picture of the ordered plates.[11]

Review of a Swiss restaurant with plant-based offer in Switzerland:
Evaluation in Points: 4 stars
Title: 'Delicious and Authentic'
Review: Very delicious vegan Rösti, very cozy atmosphere, and super friendly staff! Note: the salad dressing is not vegan by default!
Pros: Vegan options in a rural area.
Cons: Expensive.
Picture of the ordered plates.
Date of the visit.[12]

Appreciative qualities related to food, such as "authentic," "genuine," "healthy," and environmental aspects like "vibes," "friendly staff," and "cozy atmosphere," are frequently highlighted in nonprofessional culinary reviews (Kobez, 2020, p. 108). These qualities foster an atmosphere of easy, empathetic trust and cohesion, making them highly valued within these communities. They strengthen a sense of community, promote "mindfulness of others," and encourage reviewers to adopt a "caring lifestyle" (Eli et al., 2015, p. 174). However, in doing so, they also contribute to the amateurization of gastronomy pages.

Platform affordances such as tags, videos, images, and detailed information about sexual orientation, openly and inclusively covering the LGBTQ+ spectrum, often combined with hobbies and lifestyles, enable digital activism and group users into taste-subtribes. These affordances not only strengthen emotional connections but also enable detailed profiling, capturing distinct yet recognizable identities. While these functionalities collect marketing data through opaque algorithms (Beer, 2009), they also facilitate actions (Lupton, 2019; Davis, 2020, pp. 6–8)

---

[11] More information about the public details of the reviewers, the exact place, and the date of the review have been omitted to preserve the identity of both reviewers and the reviewed eatery.

[12] Author's translation from German. The original review was: Title: "Lecker uns Authentisch." Review: Sehr leckerer vegan Rösti, sehr gemütliche Atmosphäre und superfreundliches Personal! Achtung: das Salat Dressing ist standardmäßig nicht vegan! Pro: Vegane Optionen im ländlichen Gebiet. Contro: Teuer.

such as gastronomic updates. Ultimately, they create inclusive environments where users, supported by their shared ethical and integral lifestyles, feel empowered to voice their opinions and, in some cases, find validation for their nonnormative gender identities (Bertella, 2018, p. 39; Greenebaum and Dexter, 2018).

3.11 The spirit of omnivorous times: The foodies or *food-as-a-lifestyle* and the paradigm of consumer saturation

As mentioned earlier, a strategic ability to move in and out of self-control in order to experience a wider range of sensations and increase the propensity to consume, is the key ability that characterizes the "sovereignty" of postmodern consumer culture and is at the root of the persistent contradictions of food consumption, which we have also presented as one of the consumer dilemmas.

In the field of food consumption and in the definition of taste in postmodern consumer society, a term which has gained great importance is "foodie," an important sociological term designating a new profile of eater. The word *foodie* is useful for describing and conceptualizing the current centrality of food as a topic of discourses, especially the user generated discourses circulating on the web, even the making of food "a lifestyle" and a *zeitgeist*. The foodie is an omnivorous consumer, passionate about the pursuit of good food, however "good food" is defined. The Foodie wholly embodies this paradigm of saturation in taste and its communication. In their work on foodies, Johnston and Baumann (2010) analyze the extent to which culinary capital may support what could be identified as a middle-class identity in an epoch in which "while our taste in food continues to speak to our class position, this is not a simple correspondence between rarefied 'fancy' food for highclass people but a more complex, omnivorous affair" (2010).

> Given our obvious affection for food and foods of various variety and genres – high and low, fast and slow – doesn't this make of us foodies? (Johnston and Baumann, 2010)

At its rise, consumer culture was totally leaning on the emulative search for scarce goods – the privilege of élites – a quest demanding considerable investment in time, money, and knowledge to attain and appropriately handle such rare goods that come to conspicuously classify the status of their bearers. Today's consumer culture – wholly embodied by foodies and their omnivorous and wavering search for stimuli to expand their taste experience – totally relies upon a flexible underlying generative structure, able to both handle formal control and easily decontrol consumer behavior. The final goal and output of such a *machinic device* is to induce alternation between apparently alternative options and finally to enhance the propensity for consumption by continuously pushing consumers to embrace new goods and values.

Contemporary consumer culture uses images, signs, and symbolic goods that summon up dreams, desires, and fantasies that suggest at once romantic authenticity and disruptive rebellion, whose ultimate goal is to saturate the narcissistic demand for emotional fulfillment by endlessly pleasing oneself. Such a paradigm of "communicative saturation" appeals to the omnivore's innermost paradoxical tensions, by creating an omnivorous culture that, behind apparent options, rather than suggesting exclusive behaviors, points to widening the range of contexts and situations in which a suggested consumer behavior is deemed appropriate and acceptable. Consumer discernment is, therefore, not a question of a choice between two options presented as alternatives; it is rather an invitation to take *both*. Last but not least, it is important to stress that this decrease in contrasts and increase in variety did not represent the eclipse of control over consumer taste, even though such a loss of control has often been hinted at as a threat. The passage from the mass-consumption society to the neo-individualistic or neo-tribalistic society entailed the shift of control from the consumer's regular patterns of manifest behaviors (the proper terrain of sociology) to the consumer's internal yet-to-become patterns of behaviors (social psychology). In nowadays prosumer times, where most consumption is mediated through online experiences, a further shifting of control is taking place: Control over consumers' choices has shifted many steps before decision-making; it has become a matter of restless cyber-profiling of neural processes that induce emotions and genetic predisposition toward certain nutrients.

A process that we might label as from standardization, to pluralization, to customization of taste.

Part IV
Consumer Awareness and Personal Behavior in the Era of Sustainable Consumption

4   Consumption as Behavior: Between Cultural Values, Group Ethos, and Personal Motivation

4.1   The importance of values and personal motivation in times of commitment with sustainable consumption

The 2030 Agenda devised by the United Nations provides guidance in the priorities that social sciences should focus on with regard to the sustainable future of global societies.[1] This is especially detectable in Goal 12, which claims a global commitment to responsible and sustainable consumption and production patterns and advocates new desirable social praxis and lifestyles within which awareness of consumer agency is critical.

Such an objective is especially pursued through the targets 12.6 "encouraging companies to adopt sustainable practices and to integrate sustainability information into their reporting cycle," and 12.8 "ensuring that people everywhere have the relevant information and awareness for sustainable development."

Practices, *information*, and *awareness* become the keys to driving change and developing sustainable lifestyles. In sociological terms, this triad calls for the reconnection of the scrutiny of practices with the motivational underpinning structure to account for a revived activism on the part of consumers. This means expanding the focus of investigation from consumer practical competence, that is, "knowing how" which is also the usual focus of sociological investigation, to "knowing that," which means

---

[1] See: https://www.undp.org/content/undp/en/home/sustainable-development-goals.html.

making space in sociological research on consumption for dimensions like motivation, information, and reasoning that are often referred to as "nonsociological."

All of this suggests a new agenda of priorities and approaches in the social sciences, pointing not only to monitoring and eventually predicting the structuring of collective trends but also to leading, through research, to the *greening* of consumer cultures. This can be achieved by encouraging eco-friendly behaviors and leveraging the underpinning values in order to foster widespread value cocreation at the global level.

This demands a comprehensive and in-depth understanding of consumer behaviors, which is only possible by combining socio-demographic (structural) factors with deeply hidden, "subjectified" sociocultural determinants, often rooted in psychological background: attitudes, aspirations, and perceived pressure of social norms from similar social groups. Thus, while the socio-demographic characteristics of consumers are always a stable starting point for sociological research, as they shed light on the social conditions under which the population under study behaves, these structural elements alone are not sufficient to explain the lifestyles and symbolic statements that individuals make with their consumption choices, especially when they are organized as tastes and lifestyles. To understand this, we need to draw on the value-based notion of "status" as conceptualized by Weber, which alludes to an ethos and a symbolic loop of messages that individuals convey and receive to legitimize their economic privileges. Only this link to values provides insight into more enduring reasons than interests and preferences as to why observed behaviors may become "trends" that affect certain segments of consumers and not others. Values are stable constructs that are not easily changed, even when considerable effort is required for individuals to fulfill them. They are enduring beliefs that a particular state of existence or behavior in a person's life is preferable to an alternative end state or behavior (Kahle, 1983; Rokeach, 1968, 1973; Krystallis, 2012). Values can account for both group ethos in the market and, as such, can serve as predictors of individual behavior reflecting those group axiologies over longer periods of time, making them of particular importance for marketing decisions.

We live in an epoch of great uncertainty and rapid changes, in which consumers have become "unfaithful," and marketers, in an effort to exorcise the specter of the "free," voluble consumer, wholly engage them in so-called "value co-creation" by building environments that foster contingency, experimentation, and prompt playfulness among consumers (Zwick et al., 2008). Companies' competitive advantage passes through the so-called tribalization of preferences (Maffesoli, 1996; Cova and Cova, 2002), leveraging emotional attachment to consumer communities as a driver of personal motivation. They penetrate the consumer's mind not merely as a solo actor, but as a member of a web where desires are shared and shaped, ultimately profiling their innermost desires, as pursued in the goals of neuro-marketing (Hsu, 2017) and consumption's platformization (Gielens et al., 2019; Zhu and Furr, 2016). In times like these, a renewed alliance between cultural sociology – specifically addressing social research on consumption – and contributions from socio-psychology becomes crucial to investigating consumer awareness and motivation, not through brain-based approaches but through insights and theoretical framing that account for the embeddedness of consumer actions and behaviors in the sociocultural environment.

The distinction between psychology, focusing on individual behavior, and sociology, addressing collectivities, has long since ceased to meet the needs of "new marketers" (Moor, 2003; Zwick et al., 2008). Often, the market anticipates what scholars later systematize into theory. In the upcoming era of the "green deal," where research is called upon to mobilize sustainable solutions globally, an authentically holistic approach to consumer choices that promotes a less exploitative use of Earth's resources and supports the rise of ecological awareness, as advocated by Agenda 2030, has become indispensable.

Scholars of consumption, whether they belong to the analytical family viewing consumption as a meaningful act generated by the so-called "cultural turn" (Featherstone, 2007; Mennell, 1985), or alternatively subscribe to the perspective of consumption as a social configuration encompassing practices (Schatzki, 2001; Warde, 2005, 2014, 2016), or view consumption as a set of behaviors patterned through a value-based framework (Schwartz, 1992, 2006, 2012), are well aware – and can no longer deny – the strong and profound influence of culture on consumers' behaviors. There is a recognized need to engage individuals through strong motivational drivers based on long-lasting values, rather than immediate utilitarian rewards, to encourage them to embrace change.

The link to values is important because attitude towards a new object must be built on something more stable and relatively enduring value orientations might provide this foundation (Stern et al., 1995, p. 1615).

Although some practice-theoretical sociologists remain skeptical about integrating consumer behavior into sociological research on consumption, viewing it as a "nonsociological" terrain (Evans, 2019, p. 499) and advocating for a distinct disciplinary approach, there is promise in integrating research focused on practices and their structural determinants with tools developed by behavioral sciences, especially the focus on values that constitute a more comprehensive dimension. This approach offers insights into how cultural patterns influence individual tastes and desires, thus shaping consumer behaviors in the market (Kotler, 2003; Schiffman and Kanuk, 2010). Several studies have linked sustainable behavior, which by definition demands a committed and pro-active consumer, with personal values, meant as subjective adaptations of societal and national values (Onorati and d'Ovidio, 2022; Onel and Mukherjee, 2014). These studies highlight the significant role that values play in consumers' decision-making processes (Vermeir and Verbeke, 2006). They particularly demonstrate that integrating the Theory of Planned Behavior (TPB) developed by Icek Ajzen (1985, 1991) with the Theory of Human Values developed by Shalom Schwartz (2006, 2012) is effective in understanding the relationship patterns between motives for choosing green foods and the various cultural values involved.

Both theories complement each other: Schwartz's Theory of Universal Human Values focuses on the role of values as supra-individual determinants that shape personal norms and motives for action, whereas the Theory of Planned Behavior (TPB), though often criticized in sociological research for being overly tied to the rational action model of consumers, emphasizes the influence of perceived social norms (which reflect a socially shaped cultural ethos) and their capacity to impact rational cost-benefit considerations.

The combination of the TPB and Schwartz's Theory enables a precise operationalization of theoretical frameworks concerning the influence of cultural patterns in society, shedding light on the causal processes through which cultural constructs affect behavior (Bamberg and Schmidt, 2003). Integrated into sociological research on consumption, these tools facilitate the understanding of market segmentation, which today is influenced not only by structural (i.e., socioeconomic) constraints but also by complex and internalized systems of beliefs. This perspective contributes to grasping the role of values in the growing polarization of consumer stances toward societal calls for change and offers insight into the often contradictory processes of "metamorphosis" of distinction (Coulangeon, 2011; Johnston and Baumann, 2010) in culturally omnivorous societies. Such insights can assist marketers in engaging diverse consumer segments effectively and help governments in designing suitable and successful public awareness campaigns promoting sustainable products.

4.2   The role of universal human values in deep diving contradictory drivers of food consumer behaviors

Opting for organic food can be motivated by a self-directed concern for one's own health, a benevolent attitude toward providing wholesome food for loved ones, a concern for animal welfare, or a desire to respect the natural integrity of the land. However, one might also purchase organic food to symbolically convey discernment or because it is associated with the legitimate taste of higher social groups one aspires to emulate. Similarly, one can prioritize the purchase of local food because they trust "own" food, which is perceived as more familiar, better, and safer, or because they want to defend their culinary identity from external influences, or to shorten the miles and reduce the impact of the supply chain. Additionally, one can buy local food to provide economic support to the local communities that produce it. In the end, consumer behavior might result in the same desirable outcome, but the underlying reasons for it can be completely different, reflecting diverse, even contradictory, patterns of values. Why are values important in consumption? Sociology has always devoted special attention to values, but to streamline the reasons for their importance, we can say that values are the basis of our innermost beliefs; values shape desirable goals; values transcend specific situations; values serve as standards or criteria for judgment; values rank our priorities; values are the ultimate relevant guides for action (Schwartz, 2006).

We can identify forms of consumer behavior that demonstrate awareness, but they lean on different axiologies: a form of self-enhancement sustainability, revealing a pragmatic and individualistic approach to consumption, or a form of normative sustainability, revealing a conformist and heterodirected approach to consumption (Minton et al., 2018), which may result in contradictory consumer claims.

Drawing on a theory that provides a structure for motivational values recognizable at the cross-cultural level enables an examination of the role of values in the activation of environmental norms applicable at the global level. In particular, Schwartz's model of value orientation toward one's own well-being or the well-being of others, whether human or nonhuman, defensively or protensively, sets the stage for norm activation that can be egoistically, altruistically, or even biospherically oriented, accounting for variations in ecological attitudes. This can even reveal nonecological sentiments behind seemingly ecological and sustainable actions.

The theory developed by Shalom Schwartz is part of several theories and instruments developed between the late twentieth century and the early twenty-first century for mapping and comparing national cultures during a period of extensive globalization. These theories provide analytical frameworks for comparing countries and identifying transcultural dimensions for social research. In particular, it follows Hofstede's theory of cross-cultural indexes of cultural variability (2001), which was developed to address management issues, and Inglehart's theory of materialist-postmaterialist values (Inglehart, 1997; Inglehart and Baker, 2000), which addressed issues in political science and sociology related to the effects of modernization. According to Schwartz's own statement (2006), his theory emerges in the wake of these two, focusing specifically on individual differences in value priorities and their effects on attitudes and behavior – a subfield of social psychology – but it is primarily used in sociological studies of consumption.

This theory addresses the question of whether the structure and content of human values contain cross-cultural universals (Schwartz, 1992, 2006, 2012). Schwartz's theory assumes that there is a universal organization of human values and that these values form a circular motivational continuum consisting of ten items that cannot be sharply separated from each other, meaning that they are in a relationship of multicollinearity (Giménez et al., 2019). Based on a forty-item Portrait Value Questionnaire (PVQ) administered in over sixty nations, designed to operationalize various value-based constructs as motivational drivers at the individual level, the theory identifies ten distinct cross-cultural value domains. These domains encompass benevolence, universalism, self-direction, stimulation, hedonism, achievement, power, security, conformity, and tradition (Schwartz, 1992). These ten values are patterned within four big macro-orientations: openness to change as opposed to conservation, and universalism as opposed to self-enhancement. These value orientations represent the ways in which societies respond to fundamental questions or problems, and their particular articulation or combination can outline dimensions in which cultures differ from one another. The cultural value orientations at the poles of these dimensions correspond to Weber's ideal types, which serve as models for comparing with concrete reality (Weber, 2011, p. 110). For example, literature (Vermeir and Verbeke, 2006; Krystallis et al., 2012) shows that motivation to protect the environment and thus purchase environmentally safe products, especially organic ones, is primarily supported by adherence to values such as "universalism" and "benevolence," and in some cases, "self-direction" as well (Hoppe et al., 2013). This value-based ethos appears to be highly trans-situational and even transcultural.

In a later review of his model, Schwartz (2012) reduced the universal value patterns to seven (Figure 1), namely: the extent to which people are autonomous *vs.* embedded in their groups (labeled as polar locations on the cultural dimension of *autonomy* – of two kinds, *intellectual* or *affective* – *vs. embeddedness*); behaving in a responsible manner that preserves the social fabric (labeled as polar locations along the dimension of *egalitarianism vs. hierarchy*); and *harmony* (emphasizing fitting into the world as it is) *vs. mastery.*

Under the macro-orientation of *openness to change* sustained by a *self-oriented focus*, the cultural dimension polarized between *autonomy* and *embeddedness* includes, on the pole of *autonomy*, a continuum of sub-patterns of values. These range from *hedonism* (a desire for affective, sensuous satisfaction) to *stimulation* (excitement for novelty and challenge) and *self-direction* (where the exploring attitude turns into broadmindedness, curiosity, and flexibility). In this realm of values, we find a propensity for tasty, comfort food, featuring *hedonistic*, pleasure-seeking consumers. Nearby, we find a taste for novel food available in different flavors, alternative or unconventional products, or items from different cultures – overall, products representing novelty in the culinary landscape. This meets the quest for *stimulation*, featuring the habitus of explorer, neophilic consumers. In the highest sphere of intellectual autonomy, we find taste for healthy or even organic food, which features the *self-directed* consumer type.

Figure 1   Schwartz's pattern of universal human values and corresponding food tastes

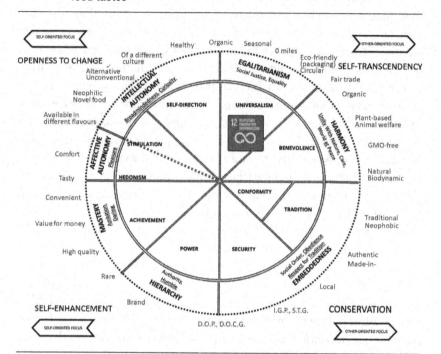

Source: Author's adaptation of Schwartz's model of Universal Human Values (1992, 2006, 2012) to the current consumer foodscape.

Remaining on the side of self-oriented focus, hedonism, and tasty food mark the border with *mastery*, an axiological dimension that relies on values such as ambition, success, courage, and competence. This dimension features an ambitious, daring, and self-assertive consumer, prone to mastering, directing, and changing the natural and social environment to attain personal fulfillment. This type of consumer, often fitting the profile of a bargain-hunter, might show a preference for convenient, value-for-money, high-quality food, and, in some cases, rare food to demonstrate their skills and discernment.

A taste for rare food might distinguish conspicuous consumers, for whom rarity often means expensive, and loyalty to renowned brands might reveal a consumer orientation compliant with a hierarchical distribution of *power* in society and its ascribed roles, legitimating the unequal distribution of economic resources. Rare, expensive food or brand loyalty may become symbols of status and identity, conveying values like social power, authority, humility, and wealth.

At the margins of the sphere of values and consumption oriented toward power, we find the taste for certifications of origin, particularly PDOs and DOCGs, which represent the strongest expression within the current system of origin certification of the unambiguous link between a product and its territory. This taste for origin, now characterized as a veritable obsession (Fino and Cecconi, 2021), leads us toward a consumption ethos oriented toward the values of *embeddedness.*

In cultures that prioritize embeddedness, individuals are viewed as inherently connected to the collective. The significance of life largely stems from social bonds, identification with the community, involvement in communal practices, and the pursuit of shared objectives. Embedded cultures stress the preservation of the existing state and discourage actions that might disturb group cohesion or traditional norms. Key values in these cultures include social harmony, reverence for tradition, security, compliance, and wisdom. As the cult of origin increasingly detaches itself from processes that attest to the intrinsic quality of the product and focuses more on evoking identity and belonging, there is also a shift in taste toward certifications of origin such as PGI and TSG, where the connection with the territory is more symbolic than real. The demand for *security* shifts toward conservative ideals of social order, conformity, and tradition. Within this reverence for the past, there is also a preference for local food, often imbued with dark, "gastronationalist" nuances (DeSoucey, 2010; Fino and Cecconi, 2021; Onorati and d'Ovidio, 2022), particularly when accompanied by a general preference for "made-in" authenticity and adherence to tradition, reflecting a neophobic and traditionalist *habitus.*

Devotion to one's in-group, respect for traditional culture, and valuing concrete relationships may result in a less conservative, defensive, and more caring approach to others. This cultural orientation toward *harmony* relies on the value of benevolence and emphasizes fitting into the world as it is, unity with nature, and seeking to understand and appreciate rather than change, control, or exploit. This approach may reveal an ecological *habitus* that prioritizes environmental protection, and mark the shift from a defensive posture oriented to prevention of loss to an ethical, self-transcendent promotion of gain.

Hence, within this value pattern, we can find a taste for biodynamic wine, which celebrates the connection with the land and natural cycles, as well as a preference for natural, clean food and animal welfare, reflecting a demand for harmony with nature and consideration for other living species. A preference for organic and fair-trade products reflects a shift to a broader, more altruistic concern for others. The adjacent pattern of benevolence directed toward specific, identifiable concrete others (members of a community, loyal beloveds, or animals perceived as akin, sentient beings) evolves into a more universalistic concern for the well-being of a larger, more abstract "generalized other" (Mead, 1973 [orig. 1934], p. 154). This shift entails an internalized commitment by both citizens and consumers to cooperate and feel responsible for everyone's welfare. This sentiment of responsibility extends beyond immediate social circles to include the global environment, adopting a biospheric scope. Others, including human beings, animals, and plants, are recognized as moral equals according to an ethos of *egalitarianism* based on values such as equality, social justice, responsibility, help, and honesty. This egalitarian habitus shapes preferences for fair-trade produce and eco-friendly packaging. Within this value pattern, we also find a propensity for seasonal food, which is often a variant of fresh and zero-mile food, favoring biodiversity. In the circular structure of this value pattern continuum, close to egalitarianism and on the side of self-direction, we again find curiosity and broadmindedness. These forms of intellectual autonomy are the axiologies that feature prominently in democratic societies.

Far from presenting merely an individualistic behavioral approach unable to adequately account for or intervene in the dynamic processes of social change on the scale demanded by climate change (Shove, 2010, p. 1277), Schwartz's model of universal human values, especially when combined with an approach to taste as part of lifestyles, allows us to distinguish, for instance, between "green," sustainable locavorism – prioritizing local and seasonal products, mostly vegetables, to reduce the carbon footprint (Schulp, 2015, p. 120) – and "black," neophobic locavorism, where local food signifies "own," identity-based, even national food, perceived as superior to other culinary styles. Distinguishing a value-pattern that shapes a benevolent and embedded habitus toward local taste, meant as a way to support the local community, from a value-pattern that prioritizes local food for ecological concerns, contrasting with long-supply chains, and from a value-pattern that "lionizes" local food as symbolically imbued with superiority and credibility – thus deemed better, safer, and of higher quality – allows us to contribute to the formal construction of locavorism as a proper ideology (Reich, 2015, p. 851). This also enables us to move beyond methodological individualism (Halkier, 2017, p. 37) and gain insights into the main contradictions of our times underlying the celebration of local food (Onorati and d'Ovidio, 2022).

These contradictions, which seemingly only reflect individual beliefs, are deeply rooted at multiple levels: At the level of consumer personal beliefs, influencing individual habits; at the level of consumer practices, shaping ranked routines and tastes within lifestyles; and at the level of political discourse, where these narratives are ideologized, legitimized, and, to a certain extent, normalized in common sense. A structure like this allows us to gain insights into how people come to combine their consumption practices into the same framework – often labeled with the appealing name of "food activism" – where local and origin often contradict each other, frequently under the guise of "authenticity." This may involve defending single-origin chocolate or specialty coffee sourced through fair-trade for the benefit of faraway local communities or consuming biodynamic wine for the sake of nature and nearby local small producers. These practices involve consumer products targeted at a high-end niche market that excludes the average consumer and often go along with the regular consumption of PDOs or PGIs to uphold and defend "own" local traditions considered superior in quality, yet primarily destined for the high-volume exports of the so-called DOP economy.

This is another lens, using tools provided by a different analytical framework, to explore the current consumer contradictions referred to as the new food antinomies in the second chapter of this book.

4.3 From cultural values to behavioral intention to purchase decision: The theory of planned behavior to capture the dispositional prediction of sustainable consumer behavior

Remaining in the analytical family of consumption as a behavior, the "Theory of Planned Behavior" (TPB) (Ajzen, 1985) is a well-established psychological framework that can be particularly effective in understanding the dispositional predictors of sustainable consumer behavior. An extended version of the "Theory of Reasoned Action" devised by

Ajzen and Fishbein (1975, 1980), this theory is highly regarded in marketing as it provides an ends-means chain model of influential relations occurring between contextual pressure, attitude, perception, intention, and action. Although an individual's intention to perform a particular behavior is a central factor in this consumption approach, and, as with the original Theory of Reasoned Action, intentions are assumed to capture the motivating factors that influence behavior, the TPB becomes necessary to address the limitations of the original model in dealing with behaviors over which people have incomplete volitional control. The TPB has become essential to address the gap between personal disposition, the intention to perform a behavior, and the final decision to act (Ajzen, 1991, p. 181). In this sense, although it is a theory of agency meant to describe individual volitional control over the disposition to behave or not behave in a certain way – and because of this, it occupies a polar position with nonindividualistic practice theories where the unit of analysis is social configurations – the theory also accounts for broader nonmotivational factors such as the availability of requisite opportunities and resources (e.g., time, money, skills, cooperation of others) that influence the final actual behavior (Ajzen, 1985). Although the unit of analysis of the TPB is the individual and their attitude as an internalized cultural belief influencing behavior by means of intention, unlike the original model, the updated version of this theory developed by Ajzen in the 1980s adds a third element to this means-end chain: the concept of behavioral control exerted by the perceived social norm. This aspect is often overlooked in references to the TPB, making it a theory of particular interest for sociological inquiry. This is especially relevant when addressing consumer awareness of sustainable consumption, which demands a certain amount of effort and volitional agency, alongside consideration of circumstantial factors that may become predictive of the final purchase behavior.

For this reason, the TPB is largely applied to predict and explain social behaviors in different domains. Combined with other theories, it has been especially used in numerous studies dealing with sustainable food consumption, particularly in educational programs aimed at effective environmental conservation (Newhouse, 1990). The TPB outlines a model of action and an actor who is socially and culturally embedded (Kaiser et al., 1999; de Barcellos, 2011; Chekima et al., 2016; Yaveroglu and Donthu, 2002; Kim and Choi, 2005).

Its integration within surveys with a broad sociological scope allows to ask questions on how individual behavior can turn into a more ecological lifestyle and what contributes to determine the rise of an environmental attitude or to what extent an environmental attitude can work as a possible predictor of more widespread ecological behaviors. In particular, the TPB allows us to scrutinize the cultural moderators occurring in the motivational chain between the predisposition to embrace a certain behavior, the intention to do that, and the actual performance of that behavior. In the effort to catch the broader spectrum of reasons that lead a person to take or not a certain behavior, the TPB posits that individual behavior is driven by intentions. Intention, in turn, is a construct that cannot be limited to simple volition. It is a function defined by three factors: "the attitude towards the behavior," "the subjective norm," and the "perceived behavioral control."

Attitude is defined as an internalized belief about the effects of taking a certain behavior ("behavioral belief"), that rises in the individual's positive or negative feelings about performing that behavior. So, the first assumption of TPB model is that behind a behavior, there is always an internalized behavioral belief that originates from values. For example, the positive *attitude* toward *buying sustainable food* ("it is a good thing") is underpinned by the *behavioral belief* that *buying sustainable food reduces the impact of my consumption*. But the TPB posits that the intention is also conditioned by a subjective norm, that is individuals' perception of whether people important to them think (or expect) that the behavior should be performed. Subjective norms account for the perceived social pressure as a factor of motivation for individuals to comply with the wishes of their relevant referents and, more in general, with social expectations surrounding their milieu. In the case of the intention to buy sustainable food, the subjective norm is expressed by the perception that *people around me would approve me to buy sustainable food*, and such a subjective norm relies upon the normative belief that *people important to me would like I buy sustainable food*. Finally, intention is also mediated by the perceived behavioral control, that is the individual's perception of the ease with which the behavior can be performed and its effectiveness about the consequences supposed by the initial attitude. Perceived behavioral control pertains to the ability to access goods involved in consumer behavior and the anticipated effectiveness of the expected outcomes of such behavior. In the context of sustainable behavior, consumer intention to purchase sustainable food is mediated by the perception that buying sustainable food is either within their control or not. This perception is supported by the belief that sustainable food is readily available and affordable in their vicinity (or it is not). The concept of volitional control, introduced in the updated version of this theory, moderates volition through internalized social and cultural factors of embeddedness, which already operate alongside normative influences such as perceived social pressure. Indeed, perceived behavioral control, encompassing perceived social facilities and barriers to performing a behavior, is considered to integrate all other motivational factors with external sociocultural influences. It is often regarded as the immediate determinant of whether the behavior will be performed (Eagly and Chaiken, 1993) (Figure 2).

Figure 2   How culture may become intention to action: A scheme of the TPB model applied to sustainable consumer behavior

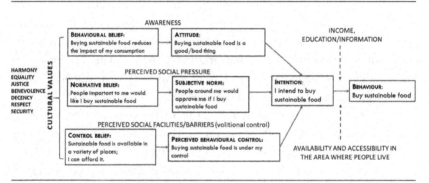

Source: Author's adaptation of Ajzen's model of TPB (1991, p. 182) to the consumer decision-making process for sustainable food consumption.

Reading in this way, planning a behavior appears to be a less linear and less purely rational, or at least less purely ends-means utilitarian, process than it seems to be when referring to this theory in the field of consumer studies. Although purchase decisions are portrayed as internally coherent behavior – at least in terms of intentions – that relies on motives theoretically within the realm of volitional control, actual motivations toward or against certain behaviors often extend far beyond individual volition. They appear deeply rooted in broader social expectations and perceived conditions within which the actor operates. Factors such as social conformity, perceived economic or contextual barriers, or facilitators, though subjectively perceived, point to a complex interplay of immediate and broader social contexts that include supra-individual social factors and cultural values influencing personal inclinations and decisions. Moreover, as in Schwartz's theoretical framework, cultural values play a significant role in predicting ecological behavior. The subjective norm, for instance, reflects the social, particularly the conformist aspect of individual attitudes toward a specific behavior, as it pertains to one's perception of the expectations of significant others. Subjective norms represent the normative dimension of attitudes, encompassing both the constraining influence of normative beliefs and the motivation to comply with social expectations and moral values. This is one of the reasons why the TPB model has been particularly useful in exploring the role of cultural dimensions as moderators in consumer behavior toward organic food products. Organic food encompasses a wide range of motivational values, including autonomous, health-driven concerns; self-transcendent ecological aspirations; and benevolent considerations for others' welfare, which may align with socially embedded role-taking expectations, such as feeding the family. For instance, research indicates that subjective norms can significantly influence consumer behavior toward organic products (Arvola et al., 2008; Ruiz de Maya et al., 2011). However, whether driven by a genuine ecological mindset or conformity to social desirability, consuming organic food also entails a certain economic sacrifice for consumers, as organic foods tend to be more expensive than conventional options. In such cases, the volitional control to engage in this desirable behavior may be affected by the perceived existence of social barriers or facilitators that extend beyond straightforward decision-making processes. Within a survey with a broader scope, we can use the TPB to trace back the internalized social and normative structure that conditions the individual's perception and the willingness to act or not to act in a certain way. If integrated with items suggested by Schwartz's Portrait of Value Questionnaire, these two models can account for the universal organization of values as more stable factors that underpin the cultural relations between the disposition to buy sustainable food, the meaning attached to such a behavior, and the actual outcomes in terms of purchase.

Of course, other classical structural variables describing accessibility and affordability, such as the place of residence or the income, can affect the consumer's perceived effectiveness, and, at the end, impact the intention to perform a sustainable behavior (i.e., buy an eco-friendly product).

For instance, the area where one lives can influence this choice, since people living in urban areas are more likely to be confronted with pollution or other types of poor environmental conditions that can influence their environmental concerns (Jones, 1992). But, at the same time, demographics alone, traditionally used by sociologists as the only elements for market segmentation, are no longer significant in predicting the greening of consumer patterns, because, in the last decades, knowledge about the environment has become widespread across different social conditions (Roberts, 1996).

4.4 Social forces and consumer values in ecological crisis: New complexities in polarizing food cultures and behaviors (beyond paradigm dilemmas and analytical families)

The sustainability challenge has been generating a lively debate in the social sciences for more than a decade now, particularly in relation to the question of which paradigmatic approach is best suited to adequately account for and intervene in the dynamic processes of social change on the scale demanded by climate change (Shove, 2010, p. 1277; Shove, 2011; Stern, 2000; Whitmarsh et al., 2010). The provocative framing of climate change primarily as an issue of human behavior, pertinent to the "dominant paradigms of economics and psychology" (Shove, 2010, p. 1274), reflects the need to consider the impact of marginalizing other possible analyses capable of examining change more broadly and within a sociological scope. Of course, it is not within the scope of this study to criticize the theory of practices, the validity of which is not questioned, as evidenced by the broad inspiration from Warde and Bourdieu that informs this book.

However, in 2024, amid a prolonged crisis following a global health emergency caused by the COVID-19 pandemic, with social life undergoing unprecedented change and individual commitment to desirable behaviors proving crucial, dismissing subjective dimensions of agency as "nonsociological" objects of study (Evans, 2019, p. 499) can create blind spots, just as confining analysis to the individual sphere of action and intention. The unprecedented complexity of our social scenario seems to suggest the way of a multi-paradigmatic analysis, which cuts across sociological traditions and, where appropriate, even disciplines, to adequately capture a new ecological habitus and change that affects socially organized conducts (*structure*) but also requires renewed activism on the part of individuals (*agency*), and last but not least, a newfound relevance of their actions (*Wertbeziehung* of Weberian memory).

In the specific field of sociological understanding of food consumption, provocatively still referred to as "food buy" in this study, monitoring a change that will be social (impacting everyday food-related practices), cultural (adhering to an ecological system of values), and global (structuring these values universally) will likely require overcoming the polarization – still prominent in the epistemological debate within the social sciences – between the theory of practices and culturalist approaches that emphasize the significance of values in human experiences, including individualistic ones where values serve as motivational drivers for behaviors. As Spaargaren et al. (2006, p. 109) argue, in times of transition, the role of human agency must be systematically considered, as citizens/consumers behave as "knowledgeable and capable actors" who make transitions possible (p. 118). In times of change, particularly when a crisis profoundly impacts individuals' lives, consumers not only participate in new practices but also emerge as "agents of change," reconfiguring their priorities. This underscores the significance of consumer agency in transitioning to a sustainable lifestyle (Spaargaren et al., 2006). It may also reveal the early signs of an emerging ecological habitus, fraught with contradictions that necessitate reflexivity to establish as an alternative logic of practice. Schwartz's theory facilitates this reflexivity, aligning closely with the sociological perspective, contrary to some sociologists who confine their analysis by dismissing concepts such as "behaviors" or "values" as "nonsociological."

Beyond paradigmatic dilemmas, the contemporary crisis and its persistent contradictions pose an eminently sociological question: a question of trust. Like most crises, the prolonged crisis of our times is above all a crisis of trust, which finds a potent reflection in people's claims related to food.

The increasing emphasis placed by consumers on food origin, authenticity, and certifications reflects a demand for both knowledge and reassurance, leading us to the core sociological concept of trust. Since Durkheim's time, trust has been recognized as the adhesive of human relationships and a crucial element for understanding societal evolution (Durkheim, 1960 [1893]). The transformation of trust in human relations has been a hallmark of societal modernization. Simmel observed the shift of trust from concrete reliance on interpersonal relationships to abstract symbolic systems as a key aspect of modernity (2009 [1908]). In his analysis of modernization, Simmel dedicated a short essay to the stylization and aestheticization of meals, highlighting how the meal, in the form we still know in Western societies, is itself a symbolic system that reflects a refinement of taste and the social evolution of trust relationships, where the individualism of the plate negotiates with the conviviality of the table (Simmel, 1997 [1910]). More recently, Giddens (1990) deepened this understanding by viewing symbolic systems as expert systems. Simmel also highlighted trust's dual nature as a declaration about the future, situated between knowledge and ignorance (2009 [1908], p. 315). Giddens further elucidates this concept, defining trust as reliance on the quality or truth of statements regarding probable outcomes, *even in the absence of complete information* (1990, pp. 26–27). Transversal to sociological understanding and theoretical framings is the concept that trust acts as an antidote to the structural uncertainty brought by modernity. *Trust* is a *concert of fear and hope*, only *partly* based on *information*, and requires *a good dose of faith* in answers. The more ontological and reassuring these answers are, the more speculative they become, with little likelihood of being verified in daily life.

How is this reflected in food consumer claims? As we have seen in the analysis of the fundamental dilemmas that shape taste, particularly during the food identification phase, a dilemma between tradition and novelty emerges, highlighting a species-specific demand for trust: the "omnivore paradox," where for those who can eat anything, everything is potentially dangerous (Fischler, 1988). The nutritional versatility of the omnivore fuels both adventurous creativity and vulnerability, prompting a search for reassuring solutions. Thus, the act of incorporation is imbued with meanings crucial to identity. These meanings can be traced back to two identity profiles: neophilia, characterized by a taste for exploration and openness to novelty; and neophobia, marked by caution, fear, and resistance to change. In the first, trust is driven by curiosity and a desire for knowledge; in the second, trust is bolstered by fear and a demand for ontological reassurance and identity confirmation. These two features of human taste recur often in the analysis presented in this book and across the many theoretical lenses used.

In profoundly disruptive times, such as those experienced globally since the pandemic, rampant uncertainty has been addressed through high social regulation measures implemented within the EU under the umbrella of Next Generation Europe, specifically through initiatives like the Recovery and Resilience Facility (RRF).[2] These measures aim to preserve social cohesion and individuals' social attachment, restore trust, and support sustainable innovation.

Social regulation at the institutional level is what we refer to as policies, while social attachment at the individual level is what we call personal integration. Durkheim (1960 [1893]) showed that social regulation and personal integration are two fundamental social forces at play in shaping the level of trust between individuals and society. According to the peculiar relationships between these two forces, social dysfunctionality may occur, with even dramatic effects on social cohesion until suicide (1970 [1895]). As emerges from Warde's illuminating transposition of the Durkheimian dynamic of suicide to the sphere of consumption (1997, p. 12), the distinct relationship between policies and personal integration can still explain very different scenarios of changing tastes and consumption patterns today (Figure 3).

The transition from the top-right quadrant, characterized by low personal integration with a prevalence of individual choice, to the lower-right quadrant, where attachment to the social group increases, reflects a move from self-oriented consumption and self-relying trust – even in the absence of clear information, as in the case of risks associated with anomic consumption – to a faith-based confidence in choices conforming to legitimate types, increasingly reflecting the preferences of the group. Embeddedness in collectively shaped taste, marking the shift from top to bottom, goes along with growing confidence, from left to right, in regulatory systems operating through certification policies for assurance.

When consumer integration is low within scarcely regulated systems, such as the upper-left quadrant of Figure 3, characterized by the absence of normative orientation, regular patterns of consumer behavior dissolve and food habits become increasingly individualized. This situation resembles what Fischler (1979) describes as "gastro-anomie," where the criteria for food habits are less socially and culturally shared. Food consumption risks becoming anomic, marked by a wide range of options in the context of rule absence. This leads to fragmentation and the

---

[2] See: https://reform-support.ec.europa.eu/what-we-do/recovery-and-resilience-plans_en (accessed on 12/07/2024).

Figure 3   Forms of tastes and consumer behaviors based on policies
and personal integration[3]

---

[3] With regard to logos included in this picture representing forms of certification existing on the market, we have used images covered by Creative Commons license for free use. In particular, for the EU Quality Schemes logos of Geographic Indication, information about the license can be found at the following link: https://commons.wikimedia.org/wiki/File:European_ Union%27s_Geographical_Indications_logos.png; for the EU logo of Organic: https://commons.wikimedia.org/wiki/File:EU_Organic_Logo_Colour_rgb. jpg; for the Fairtrade logo: https://commons.wikimedia.org/wiki/File:Fairtrade-logo.jpg; for the Made-in-Italy logo: https://commons.wikimedia.org/wiki/ File:%22_12_-_Made_in_italy_-_PNG_-_RGB_-_con_bordo,_rosso_fuoco. png; for the halal logo: https://commons.wikimedia.org/wiki/File:Halllal.jpg; for the EFSA logo: https://commons.wikimedia.org/wiki/File:EFSA_Logo.svg; for the 100% organic logo: https://www.needpix.com/photo/download/656900/ organic-eco-ecological-food-green-natural-product-symbol-ecology.

"opacity" of foods, which become unrecognizable due to industrialization, increased volumes, standardization, and long supply chains that obscure their origins. This scenario reflects Ritzer's (1998) concept of "McDonaldization," where a fast, distracted, consumerist society commodifies and standardizes food production and consumption. In this context, the consumer is overwhelmed by an indistinct, massive, yet inviting array of options that "tickle" the versatility of taste and the pursuit of novelty, ultimately leading to individualistic choices that are nonetheless impulsive and solitary. Although these choices are individualized, they tend to lack significant personalization of taste.

But it is precisely that nutritional versatility of the omnivore, which is both the source of its adventurous creativity and its susceptibility to fragmentation, that leads it to seek reassuring solutions through risk regulation. Therefore, when the formalization of dietary choices begins within a context of high consumer product differentiation and extensive regulatory oversight by expert systems, omnivorism takes shape in highly diversified yet recognizable forms of taste. The informal individualization of taste, characteristic of the top-left anomic consumer scenario (Figure 3), evolves into a skillful, discerning typification of choices through a set of rules that identify and label products and dietary styles, similar to the top-right scenario. In this foodscape, the diversification of food choices – often organized within exploratory lifestyles that embrace the exotic – becomes highly expressive of an effort toward flexible self-construction and, ultimately, an open-minded self-identity. Policies function as regulatory expert systems that, through certifications, guide the "syncretic," neophilic tastes typical of the globalized food system toward choices that meet established standards, while still relying significantly on trust in autonomous judgment. This scenario represents the reflexive nexus of the late-modern consumer paradigm outlined by Giddens (1991), characterized by an alliance between autonomous consumer agency, rooted in information-seeking, and regulatory systems that ensure transparency even in the absence of strong social embeddedness.

These two consumer scenarios, depicted in the upper section of Figure 3, represent the prevailing trends in the prepandemic globalized food market across both developed and emerging economies worldwide.

In periods of great uncertainty or crisis, such as the times we have been plunged into since 2020, distinguishing safe and certified products amid high differentiation is no longer sufficient to alleviate prolonged consumer anxieties and meet the growing demand for reassurance. Consumers' neophilic inclination toward exploring diverse tastes across various products gives way to a fearful pursuit of protection and security, as well as a desire for belonging and conformity to social groups, serving as proof of embeddedness and providing an anxiety-alleviating sentiment of sharing the same destiny. This describes the low-right quadrant, characterized by a high demand for "typification," which involves an increased need for formalization and classification of products into distinct "types" that foster a sense of identity and belonging. In this context, feelings of social attachment grow due to fear and uncertainty, leading consumer tastes and behaviors to become more conservative. Social regulations also become more protectionist, contrasting with the risks associated with anomie or the perceived "anarchy" of taste from unknown sources. Namely, consumers tend to increasingly prioritize certifications conveying reassuring messages about products' origin and labels, moving away from simply providing nutritional information to instead evoke identity, connection with a place or a community, or ensure protection. The search for the "typical," as a sort of identifying mark proliferating in a foodscape oriented toward taste diversification, shifts toward the quest for "authentic," expressing a demand for truth and origin. "Authentic" comes from the Latin "authentĭcus," which in turn is derived from the Greek αὐθεντικός, a derivative of αὐθέντης (autoéntēs), meaning "author, operating by himself."[4] This immediate and direct relationship that the authentic has with the truth of its creator, who makes it himself, refers to the tautology of the identical, as something that cannot be repeated and reproduced except in the mystified form of the false and imitation. There is something divine and reassuring in the authentic that appeals to a form of trust relying more on a demand for faith than for knowledge. Hence, when certification is no longer the classification of a type but becomes the seal of a truth, the origin from which the truth descends also gains a sense of mystic superiority. This claim for truth may sometimes manifest as a reassuring advocacy for a return to nature, presented as an innocent and healthy alternative to the perceived unnaturalness of technological innovation.

Emphasis on authenticity, as the uniqueness of what is familiar and inimitable, and therefore true, is likely to cultivate an ethnocentric my-

---

4 See: https://www.etymonline.com/search?q=authentic (accessed on 01/07/2024).

thology of origin that resonates with scared consumers' motives and nurtures feelings of in-group attachment, often with a glorification of localism and nostalgic patriotism, "flagging" the nation onto the plate. In the end, as the Chinese sage Lin Yutang (1936) said, "What is patriotism but the love of the good things we ate in our childhood?" In this mythology of origin and food authenticity, where increasing social attachment sustained by rising regulatory food policies nurtures the idealization of an origin community, we observe a process that Warde refers to as "communification" (Warde, 1997, p. 11). This scenario can lead to ideological, even "fatalistic" patterns of consumption celebrating a common destiny, where social attachment is amplified through persuasive narratives disseminated at both institutional and marketing levels. This dynamic often results in consumers feeling caught in a stark polarization between what is perceived as authentic and integral to the community's shared destiny, *vs.* anything new or different, which tends to be rejected for deviating from in-group values. This perspective confines desirable food types to the realm of community traditions and often imagined gastronomic identities, contributing to the phenomenon known as "gastronationalism" (De Soucey, 2010; Fino and Cecconi, 2021).

This explains a thriving marketing industry focused on origin certifications, associating geographic locations with an idealized notion of superior quality – a sector that thrives especially in times of crisis. In 2023, the Geographic Indication economy in the EU was valued at 90 billion euros, with Italy and France accounting for over 48% of all certified food and beverage products in the EU. The quest for the patent of "authentic" had already gained momentum before the pandemic, with a 204% increase in Geographic Indication (GI) products worldwide from 2000 to 2020, and 22 non-EU countries producing a total of 252 GI products (Figure 4). This data reflects contemporary consumer preferences amid the dilemma between fake and authentic.

In the 2020s, marked by severe crises, countries like Italy, the absolute leader in certifications of origin included in the EU system of quality schemes, have seen a shift in consumer priorities. This shift has moved away from these specific certifications toward more broadly evocative labels of national origin and authenticity, such as "100% Italian" or simply the image of the Italian flag on the packaging (Osservatorio Immagino, 2022). This trend has been illustrated in Figure 3 of Chapter 2 of this book, which discusses consumer dilemmas.

Figure 4   Increase in the acquisition of EU Geographic Indication (GI) products in non-EU countries from 2000 to 2020

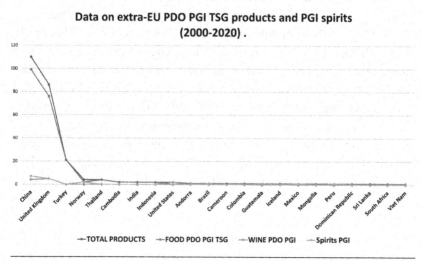

Data on extra-EU PDO PGI TSG products and PGI spirits (2000-2020) .

Source: Author's adaptation of data available at https://www.qualivita.it/oss: ervatorio/osservatorio-extraue/ (accessed on 06/07/2024).

In such a social scenario, the "shrine of authenticity," anchored in the sacralization of "origin," risks embodying one of the profound contradictions of our times, particularly encapsulated in the intricate notion of "local." The rise of communal sentiments often leads to advocacy for "local" products with certified origins deeply rooted in regional traditions or unequivocally tied to a specific place. Considering the dogmatic nature of this type of trustworthiness, these products are perceived as genuine and inherently good. However, this attitude is dualistic: On the one side, this sense of authenticity, particularly beneficial for certification marketing, meets the demand for safety standards from high-end, less regulated export markets, where authenticity aligns with conspicuous consumption and a pursuit of exoticism. This represents a huge business opportunity for exporting countries, which are also the ones promoting the rhetoric of origin. On the other side, "local" promotes a sense of belonging to one's own traditions and signifies familiarity, epitomizing a neophobic impulse driven by an ontological, confirmatory, and essentializing demand for identity, resulting in forms of gastronationalism.

An example of such fatalistic consumption is the prejudicial rejection of "cultured meat" under laws such as Italy's Law n. 172/2023, which could prove detrimental – even fatal – to future potential solutions for more sustainable food systems.

Different forms of communification, often supported by actual practices of communalization, are evident in situations where sentiments of social attachment and personal integration that influence certain dietary styles or culinary patterns are not yet sufficiently regulated or, in some cases, legitimized by policies, as seen in the low-left quadrant of Figure 3. These collective aspirations easily find a space for practice in online communities. Often taking the shape of self-organized empathetic neo-tribes (Maffesoli, 1996, 2016; Cova, 2002; Hardy et al., 2018), these groups allow for participation within communal virtual spaces, especially those advocating alternative dietary patterns and caring lifestyles (Eli et al., 2015) that demand engagement and promise co-created discernment.

Still lacking legitimization or regulation at the institutional level but animated by a sort of virtual collective effervescence, these online communities may become experimental terrains for identity nomadism (Maffesoli, 1997). In these spaces, alternative identities can be explored, normative emancipation through self-established rules can be achieved, and highly ritualized practices may lead to the institutionalization of new consumption patterns. They can also serve as initiatic spaces that amplify minority voices and endow shared sentiments with ethical value. These empathetic practices of digital food activism are likely to evolve into "heroic" forms of consumption, sometimes anticipating new trends or emerging paradigms (such as "GAS" groups, which rely on digital word-of-mouth to form networks of farmers and consumers), and sometimes fostering beliefs not credited within mainstream knowledge, as seen with no-vax communities during the pandemic. This scenario offers reflections that expand beyond a purely human-centric perspective of analysis, highlighting the innovative concept of food agency within Science and Technology Studies (STS). Patterns of heroic consumption within digital food communities are centered not only on individual intentionality or the manipulative effects of technologies but also on the complex relational dynamics of online social environments. Here, interactions unfold between subjects and gastronomic objects, where both act and are acted upon simultaneously, emphasizing the importance of holistic perspectives that capture the intricate, looping dynamics of social interactions in a society shifting toward a responsible paradigm of consumption and production.

We live in an era where all four forms of consumer scenarios coexist, each reflecting contradictory axiologies. However, following the crisis triggered by the pandemic outbreak, the last two forms of consumption have become more prevalent due to their ability to address increased fears of risk. This shift reflects a growing demand for renewed social or community dimensions, whether these are merely imagined or concretely practiced.

4.5   Concluding considerations

The reflections in this book, especially the effort to analyze the contradictions in consumer purchasing trends through the lens of major sociological consumption theories, particularly regarding food consumption, do not aim to provide solutions or remedies for these contradictions, which reflect a world in transition. Instead, in line with the sincerest sociological intentions, the goal is to understand them. Theories have been used as lenses to unpack phenomena of consumer behaviors and practices, and related cultures, all considered spheres of sociological relevance in the best sociological tradition, and to trace the social dynamics underpinning the quintessential social action of consumption: Food consumption. This is relevant especially in an era where sustainability is no longer just the cultural mantra of a paradigm shift wished for by elites but also a practical means through which individuals are urged to participate in this change by redirecting their often limited economic resources toward new consumer choices.

This book focuses on consumer dynamics, aiming to understand the behavior and patterns of consumers amid ongoing societal crises. It seeks to uncover explanatory patterns that deepen our understanding of current food-related issues. Utilizing sociological argumentation and various analytical approaches fosters creative thinking to interpret consumer trends and purchasing behaviors. The overarching goal is to highlight the potential within contemporary consumer dynamics to transition toward a more sustainable food system and shape sustainable foodscapes through consumer choices.

As readers, like the author, are immersed in this consumer landscape, the book encourages reflection and awareness about the underlying reasons driving current trends. This reflective and explanatory exercise of "sociological imagination" is crucial for embracing change. As stated at the outset, the intention is not to provide prescriptive solutions but to transform the initial exploratory question from why consumers make specific purchasing decisions to whether and how, and to what extent, we, as consumers ourselves, can engage with these dynamics to foster more sustainable choices, while avoiding the traps of contradictions and cautiously navigating the complexities of transitional periods.

References

Abernathy, W. J., and Clark, K. B. (1985). "Innovation: Mapping the winds of creative destruction." *Research Policy* 14, 3–22.

Ajzen, I., and Fishbein, M. (1977). "Attitude-behaviour relations: A theoretical analysis and review of empirical research." *Psychological Bulletin* 84: 888–918.

Ajzen, I., and Fishbein, M. (1980). *Understanding Attitudes and Predicting Social Behavior.* Englewood Cliffs, NJ: Prentice-Hall.

Ajzen, I. (1985). "From intentions to actions: A theory of planned behaviour." In J. Kuhl and J. Beckmann (eds.), *Action Control: From Cognition to Behavior.* Berlin: Springer, pp. 11–39.

Ajzen, I. (1991). "The theory of planned behavior." *Organizational Behavior and Human Decision Processes* 50, 179–211.

Aldridge, A. (2003). *Consumption.* Cambridge: Polity Press.

Arnould Eric, J., and Thompson Craig, J. (2005). "Consumer Culture Theory (CCT): Twenty years of research." *Journal of Consumer Research* 31(4): 868–882. doi: 10.1086/426626

Arvola, A., Vassallo, M., Dean, M., Lampila, P., Saba, A., Lähteenmäki, L., and Shepherd, R. (2008). "Predicting intentions to purchase organic food: the role of affective and moral attitudes in the Theory of Planned Behaviour." *Appetite* 50(2–3): 443–454. doi: 10.1016/j.appet.2007.09.010

Auden, W. H., and Kronenberger, L. (1962). *The Viking Book of Aphorisms.* New York: Barnes & Noble Publishing.

Azmanova, A. (2020). *Capitalism on Edge.* New York: Columbia University Press.

Bamberg, S., and Schmidt, P. (2003). "Incentives, morality, or habit? Predicting students' car use for university routes with the models of Ajzen, Schwartz, and Triandis." *Environment and Behavior* 35(2): 264–285. doi: 10.1177/0013916502250134

Baudrillard, J. (1998). *The Consumer Society Myths and Structures [1970]*. London; Thousand Oaks: SAGE.

Bauman, Z. (1998). *Globalization: The Human Consequences*. New York: Columbia University Press.

Bauman, Z. (2005). *Liquid Life*. Cambridge; Malden, MA: Polity Press.

Bauman, Z. (2007). *Consuming Life*. Oxford: Polity Press.

Beer, D. (2009). "Power through the algorithm? Participatory web cultures and the technological unconscious." *New Media & Society* 11(6): 985–1002.

Belasco, W. (1989). *Appetite for Change: How the Counterculture Took on the Food Industry, 1966–1988*. New York: Pantheon.

Belasco, W. (2005). "Food and the counterculture: A story of bread and politics." In J. Watson and M. Caldwell (eds.), *The Cultural Politics of Food and Eating: A Reader*. Malden, MA: Blackwell, pp. 217–234.

Bertella, G. (2018). "Vegetarian for a Day or Two." In Hardy, A., Bennett, A., and Robards, B. (eds.), *Neo-Tribes*. Cham: Palgrave Macmillan, pp. 33–49.

Bocock, R. (1993). *Consumption*. London: Routledge.

Bourdieu, P., and Wacquant, L. J. D. (1992). *An Invitation to Reflexive Sociology*. Chicago: University of Chicago Press.

Bourdieu, P. (1984). *Distinction: A Social Critique of the Judgement of Taste*, Cambridge, MA: Harvard University Press [orig. vers. 1979. *La distinction: Critique sociale du jugement*. Les éditions de Minuit, Paris].

Bratman, M. (2006). *Structures of Agency: Essays*. Oxford: Oxford University Press.

Brüssow, H. (2023). Viral infections at the animal-human interface-learning lessons from the SARS-CoV-2 pandemic. *Microbial Biotechnology* 16(7): 1397–1411. doi: 10.1111/1751-7915.14269

Campbell, C. (1995, first published 1989). *The Romantic Ethic and the Spirit of Modern Consumerism*. Oxford: Blackwell.

Canterbery, E. R. (1999). "Thorstein Veblen and 'The Great Gatsby'." *Journal of Economic Issues* 33(2): 297–304. http://www.jstor.org/stable/4227440

Chekima, B., Chekima, S., Wafa, S. A., Wafa, S. K., Oswald, A. I., and Stephen, S. L. (2016). "Sustainable consumption: The effects of knowledge, cultural values, environmental advertising, and demographics." *International Journal of Sustainable Development & World Ecology* 23(2): 210–220. doi: 10.1080/13504509.2015.1114043

Cieraad, I. (1999). *At Home: An Anthropology of Domestic Space*. Syracuse: Syracuse University Press.

Clark, T. (2015). *Ecocriticism on the Edge: The Anthropocene as a Threshold Concept*. London, Bloomsbury.

Coenen-Huther, J. (2019). "Raymond Boudon et la compréhension sociologique." *Revue européenne des sciences sociales*, 57–1: 157–167. doi: https://doi.org/10.4000/ress.5136

Cole, K. (2021). *How Producers are Rethinking Rosé in 2020 | SevenFifty Daily.* SevenFifty Daily. https://daily.sevenfifty.com/how-producers-are-rethinking-rose-in-2020/

Coleman, J. (1986). "Social theory, social research and a theory of action." *American Journal of Sociology* 91(6): 1309–1335.

Giménez, A. C., and Tamajón, L. G. (2019). "Analysis of the third-order structuring of Shalom Schwartz's theory of basic human values." *Heliyon* 5(6): e01797. doi: 10.1016/j.heliyon.2019.e01797

Cotton, V., and Patel, M. S. (2019). "Gamification use and design in popular health and fitness mobile applications." *American Journal of Health Promotion* 33(3): 448–451. doi: 10.1177/0890117118790394

Coulangeon, P. (2011). *Les métamorphoses de la distinction. Inégalités culturelles dans la France daujourd'hui*, Paris, Grasset, coll. «Mondes vécus».

Cova, B., and Cova, V. (2002). "Tribal marketing: The tribalisation of society and its impact on the conduct of marketing." *European Journal of Marketing.* Special Issue: *Societal Marketing in 2002 and Beyond.* 36(5/6): 595–620. doi: 10.1108/03090560210423023

Crutzen, P., and Stoermer, E. (2000). "The 'Anthropocene'." *Global Change Newsletter* 41: 17–18.

Davis, J. L. (2020). *How Artifacts Afford.* Cambridge, MA: The MIT Press.

de Barcellos, M. D. (2011). "Investigating the gap between citizens' sustainability attitudes and food purchasing behaviour: Empirical evidence from Brazilian pork consumers." *International Journal of Consumer Studies*, 391–402.

Deloitte (2023). *Global Powers of Luxury Goods 2023. Game Changing Steps in Luxury*, available at: https://www.deloitte.com/global/en/Industries/consumer/analysis/gx-cb-global-powers-of-luxury-goods.html (accessed 26/06/2024).

Deng, S., Tian, X., Belshaw, R., et al. (2024). "An RNA-Seq analysis of coronavirus in the skin of the pangolin." *Nature. Scientific Reports* 14: 910. doi: 10.1038/s41598-024-51261-x

DeSoucey, M. (2010). "Gastronationalism: Food traditions and authenticity politics in the European Union." *American Sociological Review* 75(3): 432–455. doi: 10.1177/0003122410372226

DeVault, M. L. (1991). *Feeding the Family: The Social Organization of Caring as Gendered Work.* Chicago: University of Chicago Press.

Dobbin, F. (2008). "The poverty of organizational theory: Comment on Bourdieu and organizational analysis." *Theory and Society* 37: 53–63. doi: 10.1007/s11186-007-9051-z

Douglas, M., and Isherwood, B. (1979). *The World of Goods.* New York: Basic Books.

Drewnowski, A. (2018). "Measures and metrics of sustainable diets with a focus on milk, yogurt, and dairy products." *Nutrition Reviews* 76(1): 21–28. doi: 10.1093/nutrit/nux063

Durkheim, E. (1960) *The division of Labor in Society* [or. 1893]). New York: The Macmillan Company.

Durkheim, E. (1970). *Suicide: A Study in Sociology.* [or. 1895]. London: Routledge & Kegan Paul.

Eagly, A. H., and Chaiken, S. (1993). *The psychology of attitudes.* Fort Worth: Harcourt Brace Jovanovich.

Eli, K., McLennan A. K., and Schneider, T. (2015). Configuring relations of care in an online consumer protection organization. In E. J. Abbots, A. Lavis, and M. L. Attala (eds.), *Careful Eating: Bodies, Food and Care.* Burlington: Ashgate, pp. 173–193.

Elias, N. (1978/82 [orig.1939]). *The Civilising Process,* Vol. I, *The History of Manners* and Vol. II, *State Formation and Civilisation* (US title: *Power and Civility).* Oxford: Basil Blackwell.

Elias, N. (1983 [orig. 1969]). *The Court Society.* Oxford: Blackwell.

Emirbayer, M., and Mische, A. (1998). "What Is Agency?" *American Journal of Sociology* 103(4): 962–1023. doi: https://www.jstor.org/stable/10.1086/231294

Euromonitor (2020). "The Coronavirus Era: 'The New Normal' – What Is Here to Stay?" Available at: https://www.euromonitor.com/the-coronavirus-era-the-new-normal-what -is-here-to-stay-/report (accessed 10/09/2021).

Euromonitor (2021a). "Top 10 Global Consumer Trends 2021."Available at: https://go.euromonitor.com/white-paper-EC-2021-Top-10-Global-Consumer-Trends.html (accessed 10/09/2021).

Euromonitor (2021b). "Trends Shaping the Future of the Food and Nutrition Industry." Available at: https://go.euromonitor.com/ebook-consumer-foodservice-211012-trends-shaping-food-and-nutrition.html (accessed 10/09/2022).

European Commission (2020). *From Farm to Fork Strategy.* Available at: https://food.ec.europa.eu/system/files/2020-05/f2f_action-plan_2020_strategy-info_en.pdf (accessed 05/05/2024).

European Communities, Council Regulation (EEC) No. 2081/92 of 14 July 1992 on the protection of geographical indications and designations of origin for agricultural products and foodstuffs. *Official Journal of the European Communities* L208: 1–8 (1992).

Evans, D. M. (2019). "What is consumption, where has it been going, and does it still matter?" *The Sociological Review* 67(3): 499–517.

Evans, S. K., Pearce, K. E., Vitak, J., and Treem, J. W. (2017). "Explicating Affordances: A Conceptual Framework for Understanding Affordances in

Communication Research." *Journal of Computer-Mediated Communication* 22(1): 35–52.

Falk, P. (1997). *The Consuming Body*. London; Thousand Oaks; New Delhi: SAGE.

FAO (2012). *Sustainable diets and biodiversity: Directions and solutions for policy, research and action*. Proceedings of the International Scientific Symposium *Biodiversity and Sustainable Diets United against Hunger*, November 3–5, 2010, FAO Headquarters, Rome. Available at: https://www.fao.org/3/i3004e/i3004e00.htm (accessed 20/02/2023).

FAO (2022). *Thinking about the Future of Food Safety – A Foresight Report*. Rome. https://doi.org/10.4060/cb8667en

Featherstone, M. (2007). *Consumer Culture and Postmodernism*. London; Thousand Oaks: SAGE.

Fino, M. A., and Cecconi, A. C. (2021). *Gastronazionalismo*. Busto Arsizio: People.

Fischler, C. (1979). "Gastro-nomie et gastro-anomie." In: Communications, 31. La nourriture. Pour une anthropologie bioculturelle de l'alimentation, pp. 189–210.

Fischler, C. (1988). "Food, self and identity." *Social Science Information* 27, 275–293.

Fitzgerald, F. S. (1925). *The Great Gatsby*. New York: Charles Scribner's Sons.

Fornari, F. (2002). *Spiegazione e comprensione. Il dibattito sul metodo delle scienze sociali*. Roma-Bari: Laterza.

Foucault, M. (1980). *Power/Knowledge: Selected Interviews & Other Writing 1972–1977*. Edited by Colin Gordon. New York: Pantheon Books.

Fraser, N. (2014). "Behind Marx's hidden abode: For an expanded conception of capitalism." *New Left Review* 86, 55–72.

Gabriel, Y., and Lang, T. (2006 [first ed. 1995]). *The Unmanageable Consumer: Contemporary Consumption and Its Fragmentation*. London: SAGE.

Giddens, A. (1990). *The Consequence of Modernity*. Stanford: Stanford University Press.

Giddens, A. (1991). *Modernity and Self-identity: Self and Society in the Late Modern Age*. Stanford, CA: Stanford University Press.

Giddens, A., and Sutton, P. W. (2014). *Essential Concepts in Sociology*. Cambridge: Polity Press.

Gielens K., and Steenkamp, J.-B. E. M. (2019). "Branding in the era of digital (dis)intermediation." *International Journal of Research in Marketing* 36, 367–384.

Gimenez, A. C., and Tamajon, L. G. (2019). "Analysis of the third-order structuring of Shalom Schwartz's theory of basic human values." *Heliyon* 5(6), E01797. doi: 10.1016/j.heliyon.2019.e01797

Giraud, E. (2021). *Veganism: Politics, Practice, and Theory.* London: Bloomsbury.

Global Luxury Survey: China, India, Russia. (2007). *Time*, pp. 108–115. Available at: https://time.com/archive/6682258/global-luxury-survey-china-india-russia/ (accessed 18/06/2024).

Gofton, L. (1995). "Convenience and the moral status of consumer practices." In D. Marshall (ed.), *Food Choice and the Consumer.* Glasgow: Blackie, pp. 152–181.

Gofton, L., and Ness, M. (1991). "Twin trends: Health and convenience in food change or who killed the lazy housewife?," *British Food Journal* 93(7): 17–23.

Gordin, V., and Trabskaya, J. (2013). "The role of gastronomic brands in tourist destination promotion: The case of St. Petersburg." *Place Brand Public Diplomacy* 9: 189–201. doi: 10.1057/pb.2013.23

Greenebaum, J. (2012). "Veganism, Identity and the Quest for Authenticity." *Food, Culture & Society* 15(1): 129–144.

Greenebaum, J., and Dexter, B. (2018). "Vegan men and hybrid masculinity." *Journal of Gender Studies* 27(6): 637–648.

Grunert, S., and Juhl, H. (1995). "Values, environmental attitudes, and buying of organic foods." *Journal of Economic Psychology* 16: 39–62.

Grunert, K. G. (2005). "Food quality and safety: Consumer perception and demand." *European Review of Agricultural Economics* 32(3): 369–391. doi: 10.1093/eurrag/jbi011

Grunert, K. G. (2007). "How consumers perceive food quality." In L. Frewer and H. van Trijp (eds.), *Understanding Consumers of Food Products.* Cambridge: Woodhead Publishing.

Grunert, K. G., and Aachmann, K. (2016). "Consumer Reactions to the Use of EU Quality Labels on Food Products: A Review of the Literature." *Food Control* 59: 178–187. doi: 10.1016/j.foodcont.2015.05.021

Gummerus, J., Liljander. V., and Sihlman, R. (2015). "Do Ethical Social Media Communities Pay Off? An Exploratory Study of the Ability of Facebook Ethical Communities to Strengthen Consumers' Ethical Consumption Behavior." *Journal of Business Ethics* 144(3): 449–465.

Gustavsson, G., Cederberg, C., Sonesson, U., and Emanuelsson, A. (2013). The methodology of the FAO study: "Global food losses and food waste – extent, causes and prevention" – *FAO, 2011. Swedish Institute for Food and Biotechnology (SIK) report 857, SIK.*

Halkier, B. (2017). Methods and methods' Debate within Consumption Research. In: M. Keller, B. Halkier, T.-A. Wilska, M. Truninger (eds.) *Routledge Handbook on Consumption*, 36–46. New York: Routledge.

Hardy, A., Bennett, A., and Robards, B. (eds.) (2018). *Neo-Tribes.* Cham: Palgrave Macmillan, pp. 33–49.

Hardy A., Dolnicar S., and Vorobjovas-Pinta, O. (2021). "The formation and functioning of the Airbnb neo-tribe. Exploring peer-to-peer accommodation host groups." *Tourism Management Perspectives* 37, 100760. doi: 10.1016/j.tmp.2020.100760

Harvey, D. (1989). *The Condition of Postmodernity*. Cambridge, MA: Blackwell Publishers.

Heldke, L. (2005). But is it Authentic? Culinary Travel and the Search for the "Genuine Article." Republished in *The Taste Culture Reader*, edited by C. Korsmeyer. New York: Bloomsbury, pp. 354–362.

Hirsch, F. (1977), *Social Limit to Growth*. London: Routledge & Kegan Paul.

Hobsbawm, E., and Ranger, T. (eds.) (1983), *The Invention of Tradition*. Cambridge: Cambridge University Press.

Hofstede, G. (2001). *Culture's Consequences*. Thousand Oaks: SAGE.

Holstein, J. A., and Gubrium, J. F. (1995). *The Active Interview*. Thousand Oaks: SAGE.

Hoppe A., Vieira L. M., and Dutra de Barcellos, M. (2013). "Consumer behaviour towards organic food in Porto Alegre: An application of the theory of planned behaviour." *Brazilian Journal of Rural Economy and Sociology (Revista de Economia e Sociologia Rural-RESR)*, Sociedade Brasileira de Economia e Sociologia Rural 51(1): 1–22, pp. 069–090.

Hsu M. (2017). "Neuromarketing: Inside the Mind of the Consumer." *California Management Review*. 59(4): 5–22. doi: 10.1177/0008125617720208

Huddart Kennedy, E. (2022). *Eco-Types. Five Ways of Caring about Environment*. Princeton: Princeton University Press.

Huyghe, C. (2023). "Wines That Stand in Their Own Sun: The Rosé Wines to Drink All Summer Long." *Forbes*. Available at: https://www.forbes.com/sites/cathyhuyghe/2023/05/30/wines-that-stand-in-their-own-sun-the-ros-wines-to-drink-all-summer-long/

Inglehart, R. (1997). *Modernization and Postmodernization: Cultural, Economic and Political Change in 43 Societies*. Princeton, NJ: Princeton University Press.

Inglehart, R., and Baker, W. E. (2000). "Modernization, cultural change, and the persistence of traditional values." *American Sociological Review* 65: 19–51.

Il Sole 24 Ore (2022). (by Barbara Sgarzi). *Fine wines: quando il vino è così prezioso che va messo in cassaforte*. 29/12/2022. Available at: https://www.ilsole24ore.com/art/fine-wines-quando-vino-e-cosi-   prezioso-che-va-messo-cassaforte-AEsvpDPC (accessed 22/06/2024).

Jessop, B. (1992). "Fordism and Post-Fordism: a Critical Reformulation," in J. Scott and M. J. Storper (eds.), *Pathways to Regionalism and Industrial Development*. London: Routledge, pp. 43–65.

Johnson, L. (2015). "The religion of ethical veganism." *Journal of Animal Ethics* 5(1): 31–68. doi: 10.5406/janimalethics.5.1.0031

Johnston, J., and Baumann, S. (2007). "Democracy versus Distinction: A Study of Omnivorousness in Gourmet Food Writing." *American Journal of Sociology* 113(1): 165–204.

Johnston, J., and S. Baumann. (2010). *Foodies: Democracy and Distinction in the Gourmet Foodscape.* New York, NY: Routledge.

Jones, R. E. (1992). "The social bases of environmental concern: Have they changed over time?" *Rural Sociology* 57(1): 28–47.

Kahle, L. R. (1983). *Social Values and Social Change: Adaptation to Life in America.* New York: Praeger.

Kaiser, F. G., Wölfing, S., and Fuhrer, U. (1999). "Environmental attitude and ecological behaviour." *Journal of Environmental Psychology* 19: 1–19.

Karpova, E., Nelson-Hodges, N., and Tullar, W. (2007). "Making sense of the market. An exploration of apparel consumption practices of the Russian consumer." *Journal of Fashion Marketing and Management* 11(1): 106–121.

Kim, Y., and Choi, S. M. (2005). "Antecedents of green purchase behavior: An examination of collectivism, environmental concern, and PCE." *Advances in Consumer Research* 32: 592.

King, D., Greaves, F., Exeter, C., and Darzi, A. (2013). "'Gamification': Influencing health behaviours with games." *Journal of the Royal Society of Medicine* 106(3): 76–78. doi: 10.1177/0141076813480996

Kluckhohn, C. (1951). "Values and value-orientations in the theory of action: An exploration in definition and classification." In T. Parsons and E. A. Shils (eds.), *Toward a General Theory of Action.* New York: Harper and Row. (Kluckhohn e teoria dell'azione sono fondamentali in sociologia), pp. 388–433.

Kneafsey, M., Cox, R., Holloway, L., Dowler, E., Venn, L., and Tuomainen, H. (2008). *Reconnecting Consumers, Producers and Food Exploring Alternatives.* Oxford: Berg.

Kobez, M. (2018). "'Restaurant reviews aren't what they used to be': Digital disruption and the transformation of the role of the food critic." *Communication Research and Practice* 4(3): 261–276.

Kobez, M. (2020). "A seat at the table. Amateur restaurant review bloggers and the gastronomic field." In D. Lupton and Z. Feldman (eds.), *Digital Food Cultures.* London: Routledge.

Kotler, P. (2003). *Marketing management.* 11th European ed. Upper Saddle River, NJ: Prentice Hall.

Krystallis, A., Vassallo, M., and Chryssohoidis, G. (2012). "The usefulness of Schwartz's 'Values Theory' in understanding consumer behaviour towards differentiated products." *Journal of Marketing Management* 28: 1438–1463. doi: 10.1080/0267257X.2012.715091

Kung, M. (2008). "Top celebrity vineyards." *Forbes Traveler*, August 29, 2008. Available at: www.today.msnbc (accessed 08/12/2020).

Lai, M. Y., Khoo-Lattimore, C., and Wang, Y. (2019). Food and cuisine image in destination branding: Toward a conceptual model. *Tourism and Hospitality Research* 19(2): 238–251. doi: 10.1177/1467358417740763

Latour, B. (1993). *We Have Never Been Modern*. Cambridge, MA: Harvard University Press.

Latour, B. (2007). *The Politics of Nature*. Harvard: Harvard University Press.

Latouche, S. (2010). *Farewell to Growth*. Cambridge: Polity Press.

le Grand, E. (2018). "Rethinking neo-tribes: Ritual, social differentiation and symbolic boundaries in 'alternative' food practice." In A. Hardy, A. Bennett, and B. Robards (eds.), *Neo-Tribes*. Cham: Palgrave Macmillan, pp. 17–31.

Lehu, J.-M. (2007). *Branded Entertainment*. London; Philadelphia: Kogan Page.

Levine, S. (2012). "Celebrity Winemakers: What's in the Bottle?" *Food and Wine, FoxNews.com*, 13 March. Available at: www.foxnews.com (accessed 14/11/2020).

Lupton, D. (2019). "Vitalities and visceralities: Alternative body/food politics in new digital media." In M. Phillipov and K. Kirkwood (eds.), *Alternative Food Politics: From the Margins to the Mainstream*. London: Routledge, pp. 151–168.

Lupton, D. (2020). "The sociology of mobile app." In D. A. Rohlinger and S. Sobieraj (eds.), *The Oxford Handbook of Sociology and Digital Media*. Oxford: Oxford University Press. doi: 10.1093/oxfordhb/9780197510636.013.15

Lupton, D., and Feldman, Z. (eds.) (2020). *Digital Food Cultures*. London: Routledge.

Maffesoli, M. (1996). *The Time of the Tribes* [1988]. London: SAGE.

Maffesoli, M. (1997). *Du Nomadisme. Vagabondage Initiatiques*. Paris: Les Livres de Poche.

Maffesoli M. (2016). "From society to tribal communities." *The Sociological Review* 64: 739–747. doi: 10.1111/1467-954X.12434

Marcoz E., Melewar, T. C., and Dennis, C. (2016). "The value of region of origin, producer and PDO label for visitors and locals: The case of Fontina cheese in Italy." *International Journal of Tourism Research* 18(3): 236–250. doi: 10.1002/jtr.2000

Marten, G. (2001). *Human Ecology: Basic Concepts for Sustainable Development*. London: Earthscan Publications.

Marx, K. (1859). *A Contribution to the Critique of Political Economy*, English trans. by N. I. Stone. Chicago: Charles H. Kerr & Company, 1904.

Mazzeo, E. (2023). "I Tried 5 Celebrity Rosés, And Only One of Them Was Worth Buying Again." *Business Insider.* Available at: https://www.businessinsider.com/best-celebrity-rose-wine-ranked-2023-11 (accessed 04/07/2024).

Mbow, C., Rosenzweig, C., Barioni, L. G., Benton, T. G., Herrero, M., Krishnapillai, M., Liwenga, E., Pradhan, P., Rivera-Ferre, M. G., Sapkota, T., Tubiello, F. N., and Xu, Y. (2019). Food Security. In: P. R. Shukla, et al. (eds.), *Climate Change and Land: An IPCC Special Report on Climate Change, Desertification, Land Degradation, Sustainable Land Management, Food Security, and Greenhouse Gas Fluxes in Terrestrial Ecosystems*, 2019 Intergovernmental Panel on Climate Change, pp. 439–550, available at: www.ipcc.ch (accessed 04/07/2024).

Mead, G. H. (1974 [orig. 1934]). *Mind, Self, and Society.* Chicago; London: The University of Chicago Press.

Mennell, S. (1985). *All Manners of Food.* Oxford; New York: Basil Blackwell.

Mennell, S., Murkott, A., van Otterloo, and Anneke H. (1992). *The Sociology of Food. Eating, Diet and Culture.* London; Thousand Oaks; New Delhi: SAGE.

Menon, V., and Tiwari, S. K. R. (2019). "Population status of Asian elephants Elephas maximus and key threats." *International Zoo Yearbook* 53: 17–30.

Miele, M., and Murdoch, J. (2002). "The practical aesthetics of traditional cuisines: Slow food in Tuscany." *Sociologia Ruralis* 42: 312–328.

Mintel (2024a). *Global Consumer Trends.* Available at: https://www.mintel.com/consumer-market-news/global-consumer-trends/ (accessed 20/01/2024).

Mintel (2024b). *Global Food and Drink Trends.* Available at: https://www.mintel.com/food-and-drink-market-news/global-food-and-drink-trends/ (accessed 20/01/2024).

Minton, E. A., Spielmann, N., Kahle, L. R., and Kim, C. (2018). "The subjective norms of sustainable consumption: A cross-cultural exploration." *Journal of Business Research* 82: 400–408. doi: 10.1016/j.jbusres.2016.12.031

Monterrosa, E. C., Frongillo, E. A., Drewnowski, A., de Pee, S., and Vandevijvere, S. (2020). "Sociocultural influences on food choices and implications for sustainable healthy diets." *Food Nutrition Bulletin* 41: 59S–73S.

Moor, E. (2003) "Branded spaces: The scope of 'new marketing'." *Journal of Consumer Culture* 3(1): 39–60.

Murdoch, J., Marsden, T., and Banks, J. (2000). "Quality, nature, and embeddedness: Some theoretical considerations in the context of the food sector." *Economic Geography* 76: 107–125.

Naccarato, P., and LeBesco, K. (2012). *Culinary Capital.* London; New York: BERG.

Newhouse, N. (1990). "Implications of attitude and behavior research for environmental conservation." *Journal of Environmental Education* 22(1): 26–32. doi: 10.1080/00958964.1990.9943043

Øygard, L. (2000). "Studying food tastes among young adults using Bourdieu's theory." *Journal of Consumer Studies & Home Economics* 24(3): 160–169.

Oleschuk, M. (2016). "Foodies of color: Authenticity and exoticism in omnivorous food culture." *Cultural Sociology*, 1–17. doi: 10.1177/1749975516668709

Onel, N., and Mukherjee, A. (2014). "The effects of national culture and human development on environmental health." *Environment Development and Sustainability* 16: 79–101. doi: 10.1007/s10668-013-9464-y

Onorati, M. G., Corvo, P., Durelli, P., and Fontefrancesco, M. F. (2023). "The kitchen rediscovered: The effects of the lockdown on domestic food consumption and dietary patterns in early pandemic Italy." *Food, Culture & Society*, 1–22. doi: 10.1080/15528014.2023.2267837

Onorati, M. G., and P. Giardullo. (2020). "Social media as taste re-mediators: Emerging patterns of food taste on *TripAdivsor.*" *Food, Culture and Society* 23(3): 347–365. doi: 10.1080/15528014.2020.1715074

Onorati, M. G., and d'Ovidio, F. D. (2022). "Sustainable eating in the 'new normal' Italy: Ecological food habitus between biospheric values and deglobalizing gastronationalism." *Food, Culture & Society* 26: 1–20. doi: 10.1080/15528014.2022.2096971

Osservatorio Immagino, *Le etichette dei prodotti raccontano i consumi degli italiani.* 2022 (1). GS1 Italy, 2022. Available at: https://gs1it.org/servizi/osservatorio-immagino/ (accessed 1/9/2022).

Overton, J., and Banks, G. (2015). "Conspicuous production: Wine, capital and status." *Capital & Class* 39(3): 473–491. doi: 10.1177/0309816815607022

Overton, J., and Murray, W. E. (2016). "Investing in place: Articulations and congregations of capital in the wine industry." *The Geographical Journal* 182(1): 49–58. doi: 10.1111/geoj.12096

Packard, V. (1957). *The Hidden Persuaders.* New York: Longmans Green & Co.

Paddock, J. (2016). "Positioning food cultures: 'Alternative' food as distinctive consumer practice." *Sociology* 50(6): 1039–1055. doi: 10.1177/0038038515585474

Pazzano, S. (2022). Vini rosati, molto più che una moda. La Repubblica. Available at: https://www.repubblica.it/economia/rapporti/osserva-italia/osservabeverage/2022/08/08/news/vini_rosati_molto_piu_che_una_moda-360868372/ (accessed 04/07/2023).

Pellizzoni, L. (2022). "Anthropocene." In Rebughini P. and Colombo E. (eds.), *Framing Social Theory* London: Routledge, pp. 39–54. doi: 10.4324/9781003203308-4

Petrini, C. (2005). *Good, Clean, and Fair. Principles of a New Gastronomy.* Turin: Einaudi.

Pollan, M. (2006). *The Omnivore's Dilemma.* New York: Penguin.

Poulaine, J.-P. (2017). *Sociology of Food.* London: Bloomsbury.

Rebughini, P. (2023). "Agency." In P. Rebughini and E. Colombo (eds.), *Framing Social Theory: Reassembling the Lexicon of Contemporary Social Sciences.* New York, NY: Routledge, pp. 20–38.

Reckwitz, A. (2002). "The status of the 'material' in theories of culture: From 'social structure' to 'artifacts'." *Journal for the Theory of Social Behaviour* 32(2): 195–211.

Reckwitz, A. (2002a). "Toward a theory of social practices: a development in culturalist theorizing." *European Journal of Social Theory* 5: 243–263. doi: 10.1177/13684310222225432

Regulation (EU) 2015/2283 of the European Parliament and of the Council. Available at: https://eur-lex.europa.eu/legal-content/EN/TXT/HTML/?uri=CELEX:32015R2283 (accessed 01/07/2024).

Reich, B. J., Beck, J. T., and Price, J. (2018). "Food as ideology: Measurement and validation of locavorism." *Journal of Consumer Research* 45(4): 849–868.

Ritchie, H. (2019). "Food production is responsible for one-quarter of the world's greenhouse gas emissions." Available at: https://ourworldindata.org/food-ghg-emissions (accessed 4/10/2022).

Ritzer, G. (1998). *The McDonaldization Thesis. Explorations and Extensions.* London; Thousand Oaks: SAGE.

Roberts J. A. (1996). "Green consumers in the 1990s: Profile and implications for advertising." *Journal of Business Research* 36(3): 217–231.

Rokeach, M. (1973). *The Nature of Human Values.* New York: Free Press.

Rokeach, M. (1979). *Understanding Human Values.* New York: Free Press.

Rousseau, S. (2012). *Food and Social Media.* Lanham; New York; Toronto: Alta Mira Press.

Ruiz de Maya, S., López-López, I., and Munuera, J.-L. (2011). "Organic food consumption in Europe: International segmentation based on value system differences." *Ecological Economics* 70(10): 1767–1775.

Sassatelli, R. (2006). "Virtue, Responsibility and Consumer Choice," in J. Brewman and F. Trentman (eds.), *Consuming Cultures, Global Perspectives,* Oxford: Berg.

Sassatelli, R. (ed.) (2019). *Italians and Food.* Cham: Palgrave Macmillan.

Sbicca, J. (2018). "Food, gentrification, and the changing city." *Boletin ECOS* 43: 1–7.

Schatzki, T. (2001). "Introduction: practice theory." In: T. R. Schatzki, K. Knorr Cetina, and E. Savigny (eds.), *The Practice Turn in Contemporary Theory.* London: Routledge: 10–23.

Schatzki, T. (2002). *The Site of the Social: A Philosophical Account of the Constitution of Social Life and Change*. University Park: Pennsylvania State University Press.

Schiffman, L., and Kanuk, L. L. (2010). *Consumer Behavior, Global*. 10th ed. New York (NY): Pearson Education, Inc.

Schmidt-Kraepelin, M., Toussaint, P., Thiebes, S., Hamari, J., and Sunyaev, A. (2020). Archetypes of Gamification: Analysis of mHealth Apps. *JMIR Mhealth Uhealth* 8(10): e19280. doi: 10.2196/19280

Shove, E. (2010). "Beyond the ABC: climate change policy and theories of social change." *Environment and Planning A* 42: 1273–1285.

Shove, E. (2011). "Commentary." *Environment and Planning A* 43: 262–264. doi: 10.1068/a43484

Schulp, J. A. (2015). "Reducing the Food Miles. Locavorism and Seasonal Eating." In P. Sloan, W. Legrand, and C. Hindley (eds.), *The Routledge Handbook of Sustainable Food and Gastronomy*. London: Routledge, pp. 120–125.

Schwartz, S. H. (1992). "Universals in the Content and Structure of Values Theoretical Advances and Empirical Tests in 20 Countries." *Advances in Experimental Social Psychology* 25: 1–65.

Schwartz, S. H. (2006). "Les valeurs de base de la personne: théorie, mesures et applications," *Revue française de sociologie*, 4 (47): 929–968. doi: 10.3917/rfs.474.0929

Schwartz, S. H. (2012). "An overview of the Schwartz theory of basic values." *Online Readings in Psychology and Culture* 2(1): 11.

Scott, A. (2011). "Capitalism." In D. Southerton (ed.), *Encyclopedia of Consumer Culture*. London: SAGE, pp. 129–133.

Scott, E. (2020). "Healthism and Veganism." In D. Lupton and Z. Feldman (eds.), *Digital Food Cultures*. London: Routledge.

Seymour, D. (2004). "The social construction of taste." In D. Sloan (ed.), *Culinary Taste: Consumer Behaviour in the International Restaurant Sector*. London & New York: Routledge.

Siegel, T., and Vale, M. (1988). "Introduction." *International Journal of Political Economy* 18(1): 3–9. Available at: www.jstor.org/stable/40470469 (accessed 01/03/2020).

Simmel, G. (1997). "Sociology of the meal." [or. 1910] in D. Frisby and M. Featherstone (eds.), *Simmel on Culture*. London: SAGE, pp. 130–36.

Simmel, G. (2009). *Sociology. Inquiries into the Construction of Social Forms* [1908]. Leiden: Koninklijke Brill.

Som, A. (2011). "Logic of luxury in emerging markets." *Vikalpa: The Journal for Decision Makers* 36(1): 75–77. Available at: https://faculty.essec.edu/en/research/logic-of-luxury-in-emerging-markets/

Spaargaren, G., Martens, S., and Beckers, T. (2006). "Sustainable technologies and everyday life." In P. P. Verbeek and A. Slob (eds.), *User Behaviour and Technology Development: Shaping Sustainable Relations between Consumers and Technologies*. Dordrecht: Springer, pp. 107–118.

Stringfellow, L., MacLaren, A., Maclean, M., and O'Gorman, K. (2013). "Conceptualizing taste: Food, culture and celebrities." *Tourism Management* 37: 77–85. doi: 10.1016/j.tourman.2012.12.016

Stern, P. C., Dietz, T., Kalof, L., and Guagnano, G. A. (1995). "Values, beliefs, and proenvironmental action: Attitude formation toward emergent attitude objects." *Journal of Applied Social Psychology* 26(18): 1611–1636. doi: 10.1111/j.1559-1816.1995.tb02636.x

Stern, P. C. (2000). "Toward a coherent theory of environmentally significant behavior." *Journal of Social Issues* 56, 407–424.

Tajoli, L., and Tentori, D. (2022). *Trade: un mondo diviso in tre?* ISPI – Istituto di Politica Internazionale. Available at: https://www.ispionline.it/it/pubblicazione/trade-verso-un-mondo-diviso-tre-36268 (accessed 29/01/2023).

Tajoli, L., and Tentori, D. (2023). *Falling into Pieces: The EU in the Puzzle of Global Economy*. Milan: ISPI.

Thaler, R. H., and Sustein, C. R. (2021). *Nudge. The Final Edition*. London: Allen Lane, Penguin.

The Wall Street Journal (2017). *How Apple's Pricey New iPhone X Tests Economic Theory* (by J. Zumbrun and T. Mickle). Available at: https://www.wsj.com/articles/how-apples-pricey-new-iphone-x-tests-economic-theory-1505660400 (accessed 20/06/24).

Triggs, A. B. (2001). "Veblen, Bourdieu, and conspicuous consumption." *Journal of Economic Issues* 35(1): 99–115.

United Nations (UN) (2017). *2030 Agenda. Sustainable Development Goals. The 17 Goals*. Available at: https://sdgs.un.org/goals (accessed 09/06/2024).

Veblen, T. (1899). *The Theory of Leisure Class: An Economic Study in the Evolution of Institutions*. New York: Macmillan.

Vermeir, I., and Verbeke, W. (2006). "Sustainable food consumption: Exploring the consumer 'attitude-behavioral intention' gap." *Journal of Agricultural and Environmental Ethics* 19(2): 169–194.

Vorobjovas-Pinta, O. (2021). "Neo-tribalism through an ethnographic lens: A critical theory approach." In A. Pabel, J. Pryce, and A. Anderson (eds.), *Research Paradigm Considerations for Emerging Scholars*. Bristol, Channel View Publications, pp. 112–129.

Vorobjovas-Pinta, O., and Lewis, C. (2021). "The coalescence of the LGBTQI+ neo-tribes during the pride events." In C. Pforr, R. Dowling, and M. Volgger (eds.), *Consumer Tribes in Tourism: Contemporary Perspectives on Special-Interest Tourism*, Springer pp. 69–81.

Wallerstein, I. (1979). *The Capitalist World Economy.* Cambridge: Cambridge University Press.

Warde, A. (1997). "Consuming interests." *Organization* 4(3): 444–446. doi: 10.1177/135050849743011

Warde, A. (2005). "Consumption and theories of practice." *Journal of Consumer Culture* 5(2): 131–153.

Warde, A. (2014). "After taste: Culture, consumption and theories of practice." *Journal of Consumer Culture* 14(3): 279–303.

Warde, A. (2016). *The Practice of Eating.* Cambridge: Polity Press.

Warde, A. (2022). "Society and consumption." *Consumption and Society* 1(1): 11–30. doi: 10.1332/GTYE7193

Warde, A. (1997). *Consumption, Food & Taste.* London; Thousand Oaks: SAGE.

Warde, A., and Martens L. (2000). *Eating Out: Social Differentiation, Consumption and Pleasure.* Cambridge: Cambridge University Press.

Wasserman, A. (2009). "Recipe for a better tomorrow: A food industry perspective on sustainability and our food system." *Journal of Hunger & Environmental Nutrition* 4(3–4): 446–453.

Weatherell, C., Tregear, A., and Allinson, J. (2003). In search of the concerned consumer: UK public perceptions of food, farming and buying local. *Journal of Rural Studies* 19(2): 233–244. doi: 10.1016/s0743-0167(02)00083-9

Weber, M. (2011). *The Methodology of Social Sciences* (Eng. transl. by E. A. Shields and H. A. Finch). Glencoe, IL: Free Press (1st ed. in German: 1922).

Weber, M. (2012). *Collected Methodological Writings.* Translated by Hans-Henrik Bruun. London: Routledge.

Welch, D. (2020). "Consumption and teleoaffective formations: Consumer culture and commercial communications." *Journal of Consumer Culture* 20(1): 61–82. doi: 10.1177/1469540517729008

Welch, D., and Warde, A. (2017). "How should we understand 'general understandings'?" In A. Hui, T. R. Schatzki, and E. Shove (eds.), *The Nexus of Practice.* London: Routledge.

Welz, G. (2013). "Contested origins: Food heritage and the European Union's Quality Label Program." *Food, Culture & Society* 16(2): 265–279. doi: 10.27 52/175174413X13589681351377.

Wernick, A. (1991). *Promotional Culture: Advertising, Ideology and Symbolic Expression.* London: SAGE.

West, D. M. (2008). "Angelina, Mia, and Bono: Celebrities and international development." In L. Brainard and D. Chollet (eds.), *Global Development 2.0: Can Philanthropists, the Public and the Poor Make Poverty History.* Washington, DC: Brookings Institute.

Whitmarsh, L., O'Neill, S., and Lorenzoni, I. (2010). "Commentary. Climate change or social change? Debate within, amongst, and beyond disciplines". *Environment and Planning A* 43: 258–261.

World Bank. (2022). *Agriculture, Forestry, and Fishing, Value Added* (% of GDP). Available at: https://data.worldbank.org/indicator/NV.AGR.TOTL.ZS

Yaveroglu, I. S., and Donthu, N. (2002). "Cultural influences on the diffusion of new products." *Journal of International Consumer Marketing* 14(4): 49–63. doi: 10.1300/J046v14n04_04

Lin, Yutang (1936). *My Country and My People*. London; Toronto: William Heinemann Ltd.

Zestanakis, P. (2023)."'Affluent and tender online': Instagramming celebrity, masculinity, and fatherhood in contemporary Greece." *The Journal of Men's Studies* 31(1): 108–129. doi: 10.1177/10608265221101383

Zhu, F., and Furr, N. (2016). "Products to platforms: Making the leap." *Harvard Business Review* 94(4): 72–78.

Zwick, D., Bonsu, S. K., and Darmody, A. (2008). "Putting consumers to work 'co-creation' and new marketing governmentality." *Journal of Consumer Culture* 8(2): 163–196. doi: 10.1177/1469540508090089

Consulted Websites:

https://reform-support.ec.europa.eu/index_it
https://www.qualivita.it
https://www.etymonline.com
https://www.undp.org/
https://roma.corriere.it/
https://winediplomats.com/
https://www.mckinsey.com/
https://sdgs.un.org/
https://www.triplea.it/it/
https://www.youtube.com/
https://blog.collinsdictionary.com/
https://www.coldiretti.it/
https://gs1it.org/servizi/osservatorio-immagino/
https://www.merriam-webster.com/
https://www.giallozafferano.it/
https://eige.europa.eu/
https://www.usaidrdw.org/
https://eur-lex.europa.eu/
https://www.gazzettaufficiale.it
https://data.consilium.europa.eu/
https://commons.wikimedia.org/
https://creativecommons.it/chapterIT/

Latest publications in the same series

Bardazzi Marco, *Silicon Europe*, 2023.

Boscaini Sandro, *Amarone and Beyond*, 2022.

Di Pippo Simonetta, *Space Economy*, 2023.

Gatto Luca, Marco San Filippo, *Export Manager*, 2024.

Ghini Roberto, Vitulli Stefania M., *CEO Branding in the Global Reputation Economy*, 2024.

Mayer Giuseppe, *Inspired by Data*, 2024.

Napolitano Ferdinando, *Influence, Relevance and Growth for a Changing World*, 2023.

Magnani Marco, *The Great Disconnect*, 2023.

Pagano Francesco, Luca Zerbini, *Standing up for the Planet*, 2023.

Patrono Mario, Arianna Vedaschi, *Donald Trump and the Future of American Democracy*, 2023.

Pecoraro Francesca, Alex Turrini, Mark Volpe, *Fundraising for the Arts*, 2023.

Rinaldi Francesca Romana (edited by), *Circular Fashion Management*, 2024.

Sinesi Simona, *Social Impact in your Hands*, 2024.

To learn more about Egea and Bocconi University Press, including publications, Scientific Committee, and more, visit www.egeaeditore.it/eng/.